# OVERVIEW

# CONTENTS

# ACKNOWLEDGMENTS

*I* would like to thank all of those who have encouraged me on my spiritual journey. Know that your support has helped me along the path that led me to compile and edit these lessons. Also, a special thanks to everyone who has participated in the Will sessions over these many years, without whom this book could not have been produced. They include Paula H., David, Judi, Bruce, Rich, Carol Ann, Susan, Cathy M., Tom, Joan, Loren, Hal, Heyu, Ron, Cathy H., Joi, Helen, Dennis, Deanne, Ruth, Judy, Paula S., and the many others who passed through our group. With this book, you are now able to see one of the fruits of your efforts. I would also like to thank the many spouses who managed to put up with us all—including my incredible wife, Lucy, who has kept my feet on the ground throughout all these experiences. And finally, I want to give special thanks to Rebecca and to Roland. You have had an especially important impact on my life and you have helped create the opportunities that made this book possible.

There are also many others who are involved with the Teaching Mission and in similar efforts to uplift this planet; I honor your efforts. Of course, a special place of honor belongs to Will and the celestial teachers who have reached out to assist so many of us in so many ways.

*—Fred Harris*

# ACKNOWLEDGMENTS

Without the rigorous and enlightened editing and the many months of moral and emotional support provided by my friend Elianne Obadia, this book could not have come to fruition. We are also beholden to Julie Donovan, book production manager extraordinaire, to Lynn Bell and Chuck Thurston for their cover design, and to Lynn for the interior design. In addition, we want to thank our friends at the Urantia Foundation, especially Tonia Baney and Gard Jameson, for their patience with our enthusiasm. Dan Young, Tom Grady, and especially John Ames were essential parties in birthing this book in its earliest days. Antera and Asana ably helped maintain the overall process of its creation. Numerous people also assisted us in the task of choosing *Urantia Book* quotes, including Bob Slagle, Sonny Schneider, Nancy Johnson, and Linda Buselli. And many thanks to those others who have lent us a hand or offered moral and spiritual support along the way.

—*Byron Belitsos*

*I*t is the Father's love that moves you. It is the Father's love that fills you all with such joy, so that you may accomplish your daily tasks. So it is with each of you, as you deal with others, as you deal with your children, your co-workers, your family. Your Father asks that you call upon him, for indeed he should be the center of your life. . . .

Celestial Teacher Will, January 15, 1998

— ◈ —

*P*aradise is the eternal center of the universe of universes and the abiding place of the Universal Father, the Eternal Son, the Infinite Spirit. . . . The personal presence of the Universal Father is resident at the very center of [Paradise]. . . . The Universal Father is cosmically focalized, spiritually personalized, and geographically resident at this center of the universe. . . .

*The Urantia Book,* p. 118

— ◈ —

*I*n ancient myths every microcosm, every inhabited region, has what may be called a "Centre": that is to say, a place that is sacred above all. It is there, in that Centre, that the sacred manifests itself in its totality. . . . It is in such a space that one has direct contact with the sacred—whether this be materialised in certain objects or manifested in the hierocosmic symbols.

Mircea Eliade, *Images and Symbols*

# INTRODUCTION

*T*his book is the first in a series of celestial teachings of a new kind. Their purpose is to unfold your awareness of a love-drenched, God-centered cosmos. They gently guide you to discover the divine center within. In bringing out these celestial instructions as they were transmitted to us, we also hope you will be inspired to drink deeply from the Urantia revelation that forms their cosmological and philosophical foundation. Each practical lesson is matched with a pertinent quote from *The Urantia Book,* giving you two dimensions of the single teaching that God, who is love, is the heart-center of each of us and of all Creation.

*The Center Within* is structured like the mandala image on the cover of this book—or like the unfolding of a flower:

**Part I, The Love-Centered Universe,** takes you deep into the center of the "blossom" to discover the nectar of divine affection. It presents a more intimate look at Jesus' life on this planet—the ultimate revelation of divine love—and gives an expansive picture of the love of the Father. It also offers a radically new understanding of the indwelling spirit—called the "Thought Adjuster" in *Urantia Book* terms—and describes a daily meditation practice called "stillness." In these chapters we learn that regular stillness meditation is the recommended way to become receptive to the Adjuster's fragrance of perfect love.

**Part II, Living the God-Centered Life,** is about the unfolding of our lives in the light of the realization of being infinitely loved. Practical lessons are given on discerning the divine will, prayer, genuine faith, learning to love, living an artistically balanced life, and family living.

**Part III, Sharing the God-Centered Life,** supports the blossoming of spiritual pioneers whose lives have taken root in the divine center within: It is offered especially for those who are now moved to plant new seeds of love and progress by sharing these teachings with others. Here you will find advanced lessons on communication, sincerity, listening, serving, and teaching spiritual truth. This section closes with inspiration for getting into action to "help transform the world one person at a time," as the celestial teacher of these lessons, Will, would put it.

## INTRODUCING THE TEACHING MISSION

*The Center Within* contains selections from the teachings of a celestial being named Will—a female in her mortal life on a planet much more advanced than ours. Will is one of the most beloved of the hundreds of celestials who for several years have been presenting instructions to groups of humans in a worldwide initiative known as the Teaching Mission. Their celestial teachings are imparted through a method known as "transmitting-receiving," in which words, concepts, and images are presented directly to the speech center of the mind of the person receiving the transmissions. These are then spoken or written down.

The story of the origin of these new teachings in the United States begins in 1991, when a pilot group of celestial teachers first presented lessons to a group of students of *The Urantia Book* near Salt Lake City. Soon thereafter, small pockets of *Urantia Book* students in over 30 known locations, many of which were long-established study groups, began receiving voluminous transmitted lessons, comprising what is today an estimated 20,000 pages of transcribed sessions. By 1993, these groups were networking with one another and comparing the lessons they had received. I for one was surprised to discover that the lessons were harmonious: What we were experiencing across the country was a unified curriculum of practical teachings. Before long, everyone could see that we had all been swept up into a mighty celestial initiative whose purpose was to prepare this planet for a new epoch, for changes that go far beyond anything we had imagined or heard prophesied.

My colleague Fred Harris is part of a group based in Florida that began receiving this transmitted wisdom in the early part of this decade; many of its members are now able to be transmitter-receivers. Originally a detractor of the Teaching Mission before I experienced it firsthand, I later found myself convening a group in Oklahoma City that met from late 1993 through 1995. After moving to California, I participated in several groups in the San Francisco Bay Area. Like Fred, I have been amazed to discover that the Teaching Mission is a grassroots, nationwide phenomenon, initiated from above. According to our teachers, the mission is actually a worldwide celestial initiative with outposts and contactees in numerous countries and on every continent.

The specially selected and trained corps of celestial teachers that have volunteered their services for the Teaching Mission consists mainly of ascended mortals from other planets in our local part of the galaxy. They have been assembled here as the front-line instructors in what we are told is a vast, heavenly campaign for the redemption of our planet, which they declare has fallen into serious crisis. They are ably assisted by numerous orders of angelic beings, who also frequently transmit teachings as well. Though theirs is an emergency mission of mercy, it is presented with utmost respect for the free-will prerogatives of each of us. The approach is always extraordinarily personal, even when lessons are presented in group settings such as the one that formed the context for Will's teachings in this book.

## A New Dimension of the Urantia Revelation

No spiritual movement is possible without leaders and teachers. In many ways, the Teaching Mission exemplifies the Apostle Paul's famous teaching that "The letter kills, the Spirit gives life." I have personally found that the Teaching Mission gives new life to *The Urantia Book*'s complexities. It is inspiring many to an expanded commitment to live *The Urantia Book*'s teachings and share its truths with people in all walks of life.

In part because of their close connection with the Urantia revelations, these lessons of the Teaching Mission have a different tenor and spirit from celestial transmissions in recent years. They are what you might call Jesusonian in quality, and they sometimes make use of idiomatic expressions from *The Urantia Book*.

We are pleased to present to you the very first cut of these instructions, as we were gently urged to do by our loving celestial friends and counterparts in this assignment to uplift the planet.

## About *The Urantia Book*

After several decades of obscurity, the important contributions to science, philosophy, cosmology, history, and religion in *The Urantia Book* are finally beginning to be recognized. In the 1990s, there has been a notable upsurge of sales and new translations. The Urantia Foundation recently announced its intention to develop over fifty new translations in the next thirty years.

One of the greatest strengths of *The Urantia Book* is that it integrates a new and greatly enlarged presentation of Jesus' life and teachings with a thoroughly modern cosmology that is commensurate with the leading developments in today's science and philosophy.

The important contribution of the Teaching Mission is to develop the practical implications of this new worldview.

To be fair, it should be noted that many *Urantia Book* students are skeptical of the veracity of these new transmissions, as both Fred and I were when we first encountered them. But after years of testing and living by these teachings, we believe that these lessons are, in effect, a most helpful representation of the spiritual essence of the original Urantia teachings themselves.

—Byron Belitsos

# The Urantia Book and the New Celestial Teachings

A first glance through the table of contents of *The Urantia Book* can be shocking: It lists more than fifty names and orders of celestial personalities, few of whom have been heard of on the planet heretofore. The topics covered are all-embracing in scope, and its literary style is elevated and complex. In addition, this 2,097-page book describes itself as an epochal revelation to our planet, which it calls Urantia. Without a doubt, this text offers a formidable challenge to anyone approaching it for the first time! A key purpose of *The Center Within* is to make the vast Urantia revelation more accessible, by providing an introduction to its *spiritual* wisdom. We are using the new celestial teachings from the Teaching Mission as the occasion for this specialized effort.

## The Transmission of Wisdom

*The Urantia Book* was authored and presented by celestial personalities and given to our world through a method that is not wholly understood. Popular lore recounts a 20-year process in the 1920s and '30s, in Chicago, that involved direct interaction between a superhuman commission of celestial personalities and a "contact commission" of six humans. In addition, a group of about 300 people known as the Forum, which met once a week during these years in Chicago, was indirectly involved in the revelatory process, feeding (through the human contact commissioners) not only hundreds of questions to the revelators but even comments on early drafts of the papers. The finished version, a massive tome, was first published in 1955, and over 400,000 copies are now in print.

*The Urantia Book* purports to be an epochal revelation to our planet; the Teaching Mission, by contrast, is a grassroots phenomenon involving localized transmissions of celestial teachings to small groups and individuals—including "live" question and answer sessions. Transcripts of Teaching Mission sessions are of variable quality and veracity, depending on the person transmitting; the Urantia text, on the other hand, is of uniformly superlative quality and carries an unmistakable flavor of revelatory excellence. The literary affinity of the Urantia text to the new celestial transcripts is comparable to that between a textbook and its oral explication. A good analogue might be the relationship between the transcribed lectures of a young college professor and the authoritative textbook his course is based upon. Bear this comparison in mind when you reflect upon the connection between the teachings of Will—our favorite celestial lecturer—and the *Urantia Book* quotes we have chosen.

The true nature of the relationship between these two remarkable phenomena—an epochal revelation in book form, and its celestial explication adapted to the needs of groups in numerous locations—is a point of lively controversy in the *Urantia Book* reader community. The celestials themselves have indicated numerous times that their lessons are designed to bring into being a more proactive phase of the Urantia revelation. But only time, and the "fruits of the spirit" of those who live out this blend of an exhaustive textbook and celestial instruction based on it can provide validation to the truth of such claims.

## An Overview of the Urantia Text

The first thing one notices when perusing this text is that it is a huge volume of 196 chapters divided into four sections:

**I. The Central and Superuniverses,** which presents the infinitely loving and merciful nature of the Universal Father and Eternal

Mother-Son, the nature and activities of the Eternal Trinity and other high universe personalities, and the extent and structure of the far-flung cosmic domains of material creation.

**II. The Local Universe,** which details the nature and structure of the "local" sector of our galaxy, containing nearly four million inhabited planets, including its administration and history.

**III. The History of Urantia,** which narrates the origin of our solar system, a chronological account of the history of the earth ("Urantia"), and the evolution of life on the planet, including a spiritual history of humankind.

**IV. The Life and Teachings of Jesus,** which contains a 700-page account of the life and teachings of Jesus—sometimes day by day and hour by hour—including a narration of the so-called "lost years" of Jesus' childhood, adolescence, and young adulthood, as well as an extensive and detailed account of his public ministry. The background data for this presentation is based chiefly on records supplied by the guardian angel who accompanied the Apostle Andrew.

## THE CENTRALITY OF JESUS

This fourth section of the book, which concerns us most here, far from being "gnostic" or "New Agey" in tone, is solidly rooted in the New Testament story. In one of five papers presented for a consultative panel on *The Urantia Book* held at the American Academy of Religion meeting in 1986, Dr. Meredith Sprunger wrote the following about the Jesus Papers:

> *This superb presentation of the life of Jesus brings life to the sketchy New Testament picture and with it a new authenticity. It has a universal appeal even when it is viewed only as a historical novel, for it is unsurpassed in theistic philosophical reasonableness, spiritual insight, and personality appeal. This life*

*of Jesus not only fills in the "hidden years" from twelve to thirty but* The Urantia Book *gives a picture of his pre-incarnation and post-incarnation experience. It is basically acceptable to all religions, emphasizing the religion of Jesus which is unifying rather than the religions about Jesus which tend to be divisive.*

It is one of the purposes of *The Center Within* to do the same: to offer in today's vernacular, through the words of the beloved teacher Will, a new and expanded presentation of the religion of Jesus. We hope its inspiration leads you to live a truly God-centered life.

# The Story of Will, Our Celestial Teacher

When I was thirteen, I rejected the Catholic Church after I was advised in a confessional that I had committed a sin against God by visiting the service of another denomination. I not only left the Church, I turned my back on spirituality altogether. Instead, I fell into a life of materialistic pursuits. I guess you might say I threw out the spiritual baby with the religious bathwater.

Surprisingly, this youthful rebellion turned out to be a step in my spiritual journey. That journey took a dramatic turn when, many years later, while I was practicing entertainment law in Florida, a famous rock 'n' roll client of mine directed a talented young musician to me. One day, sitting in my office, the musician pulled out a very large book and fervently demanded that I read a portion of it. He claimed it was a revelatory text and the main source of his musical inspiration. This strange tome was *The Urantia Book*.

Now I had never heard of this book before, and perhaps you haven't either. Although I laughed when my new client requested that I read it, it turned out that the truth within its pages resonated so strongly in me that, in spite of myself, I was thrust back onto a conscious spiritual path. I was very excited that I had discovered such an obviously exceptional source of spiritual truth, but I was immediately in for a big disappointment. I gave away dozens of copies of *The Urantia Book* and shared it with hundreds of people, but I soon discovered that no one was the least bit interested in reading it! Totally frustrated, I decided to pray for a method by which I could effectively introduce to others what I perceived to be an inspired revelation.

You have to be careful what you pray for. . . .

Not long thereafter, I got a call from the young musician who had first introduced me to the book. By this time, I was part of a *Urantia Book* study group, and he was living in Utah and attending a study group in a town outside of Salt Lake City, called Woods Cross. He now had another shock to deliver: He told me that some of the celestial beings who had first delivered *The Urantia Book* in the 1920s and '30s were being heard from again, right there in his study group—and in other locations too. They were back to encourage people to more fully live its teachings. Our mission was to work co-creatively with these heavenly teachers in teams around the country, and—like the three-part structure of the book you now hold in your hands—receive this new revelation of divine love (albeit in a "live" setting), apply it in our lives, and then share it with others. He mailed me a few transcripts of the messages, and, as with *The Urantia Book* he had given me a few years before, I found them to be deeply moving. I was so affected that I immediately hopped on a plane to Utah to find out more.

You should know that I had always scoffed at those who claimed to be communicating with spiritual personages. I figured that they were either deluded or disingenuous. So in preparation for the trip to Utah, I devised a list of difficult questions to ask—tricky lawyer questions. I soon arrived at Woods Cross, but before I had the chance to pose the first question, I was introduced to Will, one of the celestial teachers. Will advised me that she had been assigned to teach the group of *Urantia Book* readers in my hometown. She requested that I return and tell them that she would be teaching there soon.

Whoa! I immediately replied that I had come to Utah only to inquire into the reported phenomenon and that I hadn't yet decided whether it was even real or not. Besides, I said, the people in the *Urantia Book* group back home were very conservative—how would I convince them of the truth of her statement, even if I became convinced myself?

"You'll think of something," she said.

When I got home, I made copies of the transcripts of the celestial lessons from Utah and brought them to the people in our little group. Much to my surprise, when they read the messages, they too liked their tenor, and all agreed to meet more often to see what would happen. We also agreed to meditate daily, as had been suggested by Will, to see if anyone would receive a communication. Frankly, I was worried that I would be the one to hear Will. Luckily, it didn't happen; I just meditated in the silence and heard nothing.

I suppose I should also tell you that I had never put much faith in meditation either, believing it to be a worthless exercise. But after I heard Will's beautiful lessons on stillness that are presented in this book, I tried it out. I soon decided that I had been mistaken in my prior opinion regarding meditation—and about a great number of other aspects of my spiritual path.

At our next meeting, I said to the group, "Well, since no one has heard from Will, what should we do?" I just about fell out of my chair when one of the women shyly told the group that she had, indeed, heard from Will and read her first communication to us:

> *My name is Will and I will be your teacher. Rest assured that I teach with authority and know whereof I speak. Historically, the people of your world have been unaware of the leadings of any spiritual forces. They often are unconcerned with spiritual progress. It matters little to them. This group has gathered together to find the best in each other and their own path spiritually. We can but look on the future with great expectation. We look forward to working with each of you. Our Father loves you more than you can ever know. He is also aware of your dedication to the doing of his will and urges you to daily seek his will in your lives. Take time every day to call upon God and his guidance. He will always be there with you. Be responsive to his guidance in all things and he will show you the way.*

That was the beginning of our celestial contact.

I was personally present as a lengthy series of lessons—along with plenty of time for questions—was transmitted to our group in Florida, which for the last six-and-a-half years has met virtually every week. The result is that not only has my life and perspective completely changed, but we now have on our hands nearly one thousand transcript pages of celestial teachings. Byron and I have distilled the essence of these lessons, and we are pleased to offer you here a compilation of the most inspiring of Will's teachings, accompanied by quotes from *The Urantia Book*.

This book is our way of introducing a series of volumes on this celestially inspired mission. Whether or not you believe that these lessons were celestially imparted, I hope that you will find them of assistance in your effort to make sense of life on this planet. As Will has often advised us:

> *All spiritual teachings must be evaluated by their content, and not followed or rejected because of the celebrity of their supposed source. The time is long past on this planet when spiritual seeking can be promulgated by asserting the authority of the teacher. It must be the teachings themselves and the effect they have on the students' lives and not the claimed authority of their source that must be the final determinant in evaluating any spiritual teaching.*

*The Urantia Book* gives similar advice, in these words of Jesus:

> *You must cease to seek for the word of God only on the pages of the olden records of theologic authority. Those who are born of the spirit of God shall henceforth discern the word of God regardless of whence it appears to take origin. Divine truth must not be discounted because the channel of its bestowal is apparently human. Many of your brethren have minds which accept the theory of God while they spiritually fail to realize the presence of God. And that is just the reason why I have so often taught you that the kingdom of heaven can best be realized by acquiring the spiritual attitude of a sincere child. It is not the*

*mental immaturity of the child that I commend to you but rather the spiritual simplicity of such an easy-believing and fully-trusting little one. It is not so important that you should know about the fact of God as that you should increasingly grow in the ability to feel the presence of God.*

*When you once begin to find God in your soul, presently you will begin to discover him in other men's souls and eventually in all the creatures and creations of a mighty universe. But what chance does the Father have to appear as a God of supreme loyalties and divine ideals in the souls of men who give little or no time to the thoughtful contemplation of such eternal realities?*

—*The Urantia Book*, pp. 1732–33

Will's lessons in this book have provided me with reliable guidance for my spiritual path. It is my sincere hope that her teachings will prove equally meaningful for you.

—*Fred Harris*

# PART I

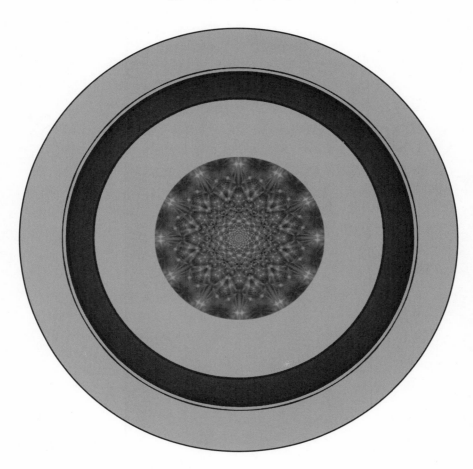

# THE LOVE-CENTERED UNIVERSE

# CHAPTER 1

# JESUS' LIFE WAS A DISCLOSURE OF LOVE

# JESUS LISTENED WITH HIS HEART

*J*esus, when he lived and walked on this world, experienced life at its fullest. He knew the heartache that so many of you suffer on this world. He knew the pain of losing a loved one, the distress of not being understood by his family members. He lived as deeply as he could so that in his incarnation experience he would fully understand your pain and distress.

He was, among other things, a master storyteller; he could weave stories that wrapped around the minds and hearts of those who listened and held them enraptured. Yet greater even than that was his ability to listen, to open his heart to his fellow sojourners and allow them to open theirs. He led them, with a simple word or two, so that what they held within their hearts could spill out. With well-placed questions, he would allow others, often strangers, to tell their stories and bare their hearts to him.

He had no need of a verbalization of what they held within their hearts, for indeed, he knew. And yet in the telling was a connection made between the child and the Creator, between brothers, between friends. Instantly, before a word was spoken, he knew

20

*J*esus' usual technique of social contact was to draw people out and into talking with him by asking them questions. The interview would usually begin by his asking them questions and end by their asking him questions. He was equally adept in teaching by either asking or answering questions. As a rule, to those he taught the most, he said the least. Those who derived most benefit from his personal ministry were overburdened, anxious, and dejected mortals who gained much relief because of the opportunity to unburden their souls to a sympathetic and understanding listener, and he was all that and more.

—*The Urantia Book,* pp. 1460–61

and understood their needs. He could have shortened the entire process by cutting directly to the chase, to use your vernacular. And yet he understood the need of his children to bare their hearts, for in doing so, their pain and distress were alleviated.

# JESUS CONCERNED HIMSELF ONLY WITH FUNDAMENTALS

**W**e often wonder how it is that Jesus could live an absolutely blameless life. How is it that his life could perfectly conform to the will of the heavenly Father? The answer to these questions is deceptively simple. He could do so because he never concerned himself with superficial matters. When any choice among multiple options presented itself, he concerned himself with only the fundamental issue—determining which path most closely conformed with the will of the Father in heaven. We feel that this technique is of great value and import to you all.

The basic rule that we divine from the circumstances of Jesus is this: By concerning himself only with the fundamentals, he never made a mistake. By having as his source of true concern only the

*I*n a religious genius, strong spiritual faith so many times leads directly to disastrous fanaticism, to exaggeration of the religious ego, but it was not so with Jesus. He was not unfavorably affected in his practical life by his extraordinary faith and spirit attainment because this spiritual exaltation was a wholly unconscious and spontaneous soul expression of his personal experience with God.

The all-consuming and indomitable spiritual faith of Jesus never became fanatical, for it never attempted to run away with his well-balanced intellectual judgments concerning the proportional values of practical and commonplace social, economic, and moral life situations. The Son of Man was a splendidly unified human personality; he was a perfectly endowed divine being; he was also magnificently co-ordinated as a combined human and divine being functioning on earth as a single personality. Always did the Master co-ordinate the faith of the soul with the wisdom-appraisals of seasoned experience.

—*The Urantia Book*, p. 2088

discovery of the Father's will, he was assured that he would never stray from the path. This technique is open to you. We encourage you to embrace it. Incorporate it into your daily lives, into your dealings with your friends, with your enemies, with strangers, and with family.

# JUST LIKE YOU, JESUS HAD TO PRACTICE

**Y**ou have asked whether Jesus of Nazareth had some particular ability that allowed him to communicate on a spiritual level with his associates, or whether, like you, he began roughly and made steady progress. The short answer is that he had no more ability than any other person on this planet. That was basic to the requirements of his mission. However, as a youth, he had many opportunities to speak with people who traveled through Nazareth, because his home was on the outskirts of town. Many people stopped by, if only to ask to water their stock or partake of water themselves, so he often had occasion to talk with people who traveled the roads of the Near East. This is where he began to develop his curiosity about the greater world outside the confines of his village. But the main point is this: Just like you, he had to practice.

**I**t is literally true that the creative Word—the Creator Son—of the Universal Father was "made flesh and dwelt as a man of the realm on Urantia." He labored, grew weary, rested, and slept. He hungered and satisfied such cravings with food; he thirsted and quenched his thirst with water. He experienced the full gamut of human feelings and emotions; he was "in all things tested, even as you are," and he suffered and died.

He obtained knowledge, gained experience, and combined these into wisdom, just as do other mortals of the realm. Until after his baptism he availed himself of no supernatural power. He employed no agency not a part of his human endowment as a son of Joseph and Mary.

As to the attributes of his prehuman existence, he emptied himself. Prior to the beginning of his public work his knowledge of men and events was wholly self-limited. He was a true man among men.

— *The Urantia Book,* pp. 1407–8

# THE ATONEMENT DOCTRINE IS OUTDATED

**W**hile the biblical concept of atonement is rationally and emotionally satisfying, you who have benefited from a more advanced teaching can see that atonement is a rather primitive explanation for the significance of the death of Jesus of Nazareth.

The people of your planet, even only a thousand years ago, were mentally unable to grasp the true story of the man, no matter how inspiring. They lacked not only the mental capacity but also the necessary social capacity, for nothing like this man's life existed in the huts and stone halls of the high- and low-born of the West. Therefore, the gift became an icon—an item impossible to

**W**hen once you grasp the idea of God as a true and loving Father, the only concept which Jesus ever taught, you must forthwith, in all consistency, utterly abandon all those primitive notions about God as an offended monarch, a stern and all-powerful ruler whose chief delight is to detect his subjects in wrongdoing and to see that they are adequately punished, unless some being almost equal to himself should volunteer to suffer for them, to die as a substitute and in their stead. The whole idea of ransom and atonement is incompatible with the concept of God as it was taught and exemplified by Jesus of Nazareth. The infinite love of God is not secondary to anything in the divine nature.

All of this concept of atonement and sacrificial salvation is rooted and grounded in selfishness. Jesus taught that *service* to one's fellows is the highest concept of the brotherhood of spirit believers. Salvation should be taken for granted by those who believe in the fatherhood of God. The believer's chief concern should not be the selfish desire for personal salvation but rather the unselfish urge to love and, therefore, serve one's fellows even as Jesus loved and served mortal men.

—*The Urantia Book*, p. 2017

understand, revered for the very quality that made it inaccessible to the minds of the humans who were intended to be its chief beneficiaries. For the man Jesus lived and died as a man not only for the people of your world but also for the other worlds, both light and dim, in this universe.[1]

The doctrine of atonement is a trivialization of the events that took place on your world. This may be difficult for some to grasp, for atonement has a neatness to it that is mightily appealing. The primary lure is its inherent ability to keep God remote and safely distant in historic times—not applicable or relevant to your daily lives.

This is error. God lives in you, through you, with you. His presence is all-pervasive throughout Creation. The concept of atonement leads immediately to the deduction that God cares only so much, and that otherwise humans are on their own. This is untrue. The Father participates on a moment-to-moment basis. There is no reflective time lag in the Father's presence. He does not hitchhike on your perceptions, he is on the cutting edge—where life can be most fearsome, and also most exhilarating. That is where the growth takes place. This is why we have asked you in your group exercises to take risks, so that you can feel the presence of the Father in the vitality of the immediate presence of humanity at its finest—spontaneous, unguarded, truthful, brave . . . and cowardly. That is where the progress takes place.

---

[1] "This universe" refers to the local universe of ten million planets. In the glossary, see "Nebadon."

# THE RESURRECTION REVEALED THE TRUTH OF JESUS' TEACHINGS

On this anniversary of the resurrection of our Creator Son Christ Michael,[1] let us take time to recognize the magnitude of his gift to this planet. Urantia[2] is a star in the local universe[3] and will always hold a place of special recognition because of Michael's bestowal here. But the greatest gift is to the mortals of this planet.

Michael lived the life of a human, with all its varied experiences. No one knows this life better than he does. Whenever you feel weakness overcoming you, whenever faith becomes hard to grasp as you feel overwhelmed by human existence, Michael will be there for you. He knows your pain, weaknesses, and strengths better than you know them yourself. Let him help you. He lived his life on this planet and he is very capable of understanding your needs; you have but to ask. His life on Urantia is a cause for celebration on many planes beyond your own. Many of us still feel wonder and awe at this selfless act of our Creator Son.

Michael understands your troubles and travails. He himself lived the full range: was born, lived the life of a mortal on this planet, and died. He understands your situation, as only one who has himself walked in your shoes could understand. His loving presence is with you always, ready to assist at a moment's request.

Today marks the day when Christ Michael showed to this

To "follow Jesus" means to personally share his religious faith and to enter into the spirit of the Master's life of unselfish service for man. One of the most important things in human living is to find out what Jesus believed, to discover his ideals, and to strive for the achievement of his exalted life purpose. Of all human knowledge, that which is of greatest value is to know the religious life of Jesus and how he lived it.

—*The Urantia Book,* p. 2090

world the truth of his teachings. When he, in his glorified form, appeared to his former family, friends, acquaintances, apostles, and disciples, his message was to go forth and preach the good news that we are all children of a loving God. Therefore, brothers and sisters, we are to exhibit his teachings in our everyday lives. We are to be transformed and go forth to all nations and peoples with the good news of the Kingdom of Heaven, where entrance is attained by faith.

And so we again today rejoice at the fulfillment of the Master's promise to return. But let us not overlook his message to our brethren. Let us not be caught up in the excitement of his resurrection and forget his call for all of us to be about the Father's work. All heaven rejoices in such a merciful and loving Creator Son who chose to live among you and to drink the bitter cup as a prelude to the glorious resurrection.

---

[1] Jesus Christ is known by the name "Michael" or "Christ Michael" in *The Urantia Book*. See "Christ Michael" and "Creator Son" in the glossary.

[2] "Urantia" is the name of our planet according to the *Urantia* text.

[3] See "local universe" in the glossary.

# CHAPTER 2

# REALIZATIONS OF THE FATHER'S LOVE

*C*all on the love of the Father. Nothing would exist except for his desire to share himself. He is truly the First Source and the Center of all that is. His love flows out like a river. All who are bold enough to set forth within it are washed clean. A truer and purer love exists nowhere. The Father's love washes out over all the worlds, over each life. It finds its expression in the relationship between people, between parent and child, even in the soft touch of affection between a human and an animal.

*T*he love of the Father absolutely individualizes each personality as a unique child of the Universal Father, a child without duplicate in infinity, a will creature irreplaceable in all eternity. The Father's love glorifies each child of God, illuminating each member of the celestial family, sharply silhouetting the unique nature of each personal being against the impersonal levels that lie outside the fraternal circuit of the Father of all. The love of God strikingly portrays the transcendent value of each will creature, unmistakably reveals the high value which the Universal Father has placed upon each and every one of his children from the highest creator personality of Paradise status to the lowest personality of will dignity among the savage tribes of men in the dawn of the human species on some evolutionary world of time and space.

—*The Urantia Book,* p. 138

# GOD WORKS WITH YOU ONLY IN THE PRESENT

God is capable of working directly with you only when you live in the present. It is one of the problems of modern life—you tend not to live in the present moment. Some choose the past, some see only the future, but virtually all deny the immediacy of the present. And yet the present is all that is. Without a present, there is neither future nor past.

Try to live in the present. That is where life is. That is where God's love is. God cannot love you in the past. God cannot love you in the future—although it is certain that he will. The future is in a state of becoming; it is not a fact of universal life. God's love is right now. Try to open yourself to it. In the stressful times, when emotions run high and your lives seem like a mess of things yet to be done, things undone, and missed chances, let the love of God fill your lives and wash away the problems.

To become mature is to live more intensely in the present, at the same time escaping from the limitations of the present. The plans of maturity, founded on past experience, are coming into being in the present in such manner as to enhance the values of the future.

The time unit of immaturity concentrates meaning-value into the present moment in such a way as to divorce the present of its true relationship to the not-present—the past-future. The time unit of maturity is proportioned so to reveal the co-ordinate relationship of past-present-future that the self begins to gain insight into the wholeness of events, begins to view the landscape of time from the panoramic perspective of broadened horizons, begins perhaps to suspect the nonbeginning, nonending eternal continuum, the fragments of which are called time.

—*The Urantia Book*, pp. 1295–96

I pride myself on the quality of my companionship, but there is no companion like the Father. The Father will never leave you, although many times you may leave the Father. His love is secure. It is the perfect straight arrow—a beam of light that never bends, never stops. As far as we know, it has no beginning. It has no end. It is perfect.

# THIS PLANET IS BEING SUPER-CHARGED WITH THE FATHER'S LOVE

The love of the Father surrounds us, filling our hearts with his light, inspiring us to aspire to ever closer connection with him. The beauty of the Father lightens our hearts, filling us with a sense of wonder and awe to give our souls, our minds, and our hearts respite from the wearying burdens that a life on this planet engenders. The power of the Father lifts us up, supporting us when we would fall but for his support. Wherever we are, he is.

All who live upon this planet live and work in an atmosphere that is being supercharged with the Father's love. All who yearn for their connection with the Father are being supported and surrounded by those who would help them find their way. It is true that it takes many years before Light and Life[1] on any world is an accomplished fact, but on a world such as yours, where so much has gone awry, the time it will take for Light and Life to be fully established is much longer, using your years as a measure. And yet from a more universal perspective, it is happening very quickly.

Many there are across this planet—myriad groups of people as well as individuals working alone—who, because of the work they are doing and the openness of their minds and hearts to the incoming flow of light from the Father, are beginning to experience Light and Life within the framework of their lives. This happens one by one. And as these light workers allow their light to

While you cannot observe the divine spirit at work in your minds, there is a practical method of discovering the degree to which you have yielded the control of your soul powers to the teaching and guidance of this indwelling spirit of the heavenly Father, and that is the degree of your love for your fellow men.
—Jesus to the Apostle Thomas, *The Urantia Book,* p. 1642

shine ever more brightly and allow the Father to reach out to those within the arena of their lives, the numbers increase. The energy coming into your planet is working with individuals on many levels simultaneously.

If you had any idea of the energy, the Father's energy—this loving force for change that is loosed upon this planet through you—you would indeed be amazed. We understand that as yet you may not recognize the work you do. You may not yet understand that when you allow yourselves to become a conduit, a living, loving conduit for the Father's outreach, you, in a brief exchange with another, allow a connection to be made—an active, living connection that exists for but a brief moment between you and your sibling, allowing the Father to open the mind and the heart and to plant the seeds that will in future days grow up and blossom toward him. This is the work you all accomplish in those chance encounters we have been asking you to seek. A smile, a kindly spoken word—these are the keys that open the hearts of all who receive the gift of love from you.

[1] "Light and Life" is the era of universal enlightenment on all inhabited planets.

# ONE BY ONE, ALL HEARTS
# WILL TURN TO GOD

The Father in Heaven is personally concerned with the daily events that occur in the lives of his independent-minded free-will creatures. It is the most important relationship in all of Creation. The Father learns things from us that he could not otherwise know. And the human learns that where God is a constant companion, there is no such thing as isolation.

There is no love as true as the Father's love. No matter what happens in your daily life, the Universal Father feels what you feel, hurts when you hurt, laughs when you laugh, loves when you love. Except for you, he would never experience these feelings in just the same way; that is why he made you different from every other person in the world.

God's plan favors variety over conformity. That makes life more difficult for humans, but he thinks we are equal to the task, for he also gave us talents to deal with the problems we face.

God has asked that the people of this world no longer live in the shadow of political and economic exploitation. The skills of the exploiters have become so refined, so scientifically sound, that the Word of God is in danger of being rubbed out, and children not yet born will be defenseless against the forces of commercial tyranny.

Life has little to do with material, worldly success. The only benefit of progress that has value in God's eyes is the free time that is created. Yet too many people of your world do virtually nothing

The religion of the kingdom is personal, individual; the fruits, the results, are familial, social. Jesus never failed to exalt the sacredness of the individual as contrasted with the community.
—*The Urantia Book*, p. 1862

with free time except conspire to more ruthlessly exploit their weaker-minded brothers and sisters.

This situation must change and, under the laws of spiritual progress, the change must take place in human hearts, one person at a time. One by one, the hearts of men and women on your planet will turn to God, for he is the only answer to the problems you see all around you. He is the answer to the problems you face within yourself and he is the answer to each level of the problems you face as you raise your view to the outside world—your neighborhood, town, nation, and planet.

All will be resolved, brought back within the fold, not by new organizations yet to be formed but by the actions and mind changes of individual humans.

# THE FATHER'S LOVE IS A FLAME

The campfires of your world, whether on the plain or in the forest, warm their visitors on one side only. But when you stand by the fire of the Father's love, it warms you through and through. The Father's flame is a flame that you may carry with you in your hearts no matter how far you travel from your source of fuel. You may share its warmth with all whom you encounter. Just as a flame transfers itself from one fire to another, so shall the Father's flame transfer itself from one heart to another. Nothing more is required from each of you than a degree of proximity. We ask that you approach near enough to your neighbors that the Father's flame is allowed to pass between you.

All true love is from God, and man receives the divine affection as he himself bestows this love upon his fellows. Love is dynamic. It can never be captured; it is alive, free, thrilling, and always moving. Man can never take the love of the Father and imprison it within his heart. The Father's love can become real to mortal man only by passing through that man's personality as he in turn bestows this love upon his fellows. The great circuit of love is from the Father, through sons to brothers, and hence to the Supreme.

—*The Urantia Book,* p. 1289

# CHAPTER 3

# THE INDWELLING SPIRIT: INFINITE GIFT OF LOVE

# A BRILLIANT SPARK OF GOD IS BESTOWED UPON YOU

God's gifts to you all are not ready-made, like custom-tailored clothes, to be immediately used at full speed. Rather, everything on the material worlds—everything—begins as coarse material, to be hammered into rough-and-ready shape, maybe usable, maybe not. It is like being dropped off in a wilderness. Depending on chance circumstances, some find themselves with a nearly complete tool kit, plans and materials at hand. Even then, among those so favored, many begin looking around for someone to build their house for them.

Others, less favored, begin with only a crude idea—some dim remembrance of the race intellect—of which way to proceed. Then they set about roughing out the tools, the shelter, the life to be lived, and improve as they can with the spare time created. Among these, too, some cast about for others less fortunate, to press them into ungrateful and unproductive service, exploiting their brothers rudely.

And last, there are the truly unfortunate, the defectives, the genetically impaired, those damaged in the tragedies of the evolutionary worlds,[1] with nothing in their kit but the spirit of life. They have the means to accomplish little beyond survival. Yet they

However Urantia mortals may differ in their intellectual, social, economic, and even moral opportunities and endowments, forget not that their spiritual endowment is uniform and unique. They all enjoy the same divine presence of the gift from the Father, and they are all equally privileged to seek intimate personal communion with this indwelling spirit of divine origin, while they may all equally choose to accept the uniform spiritual leading of these Mystery Monitors.[2]

—*The Urantia Book*, p. 63

are not adrift, no matter what the unlucky chance of their circumstance, for the Father sees not the accidents of birth. He sees only
the progress, the indications of new direction, and the reception of
his love and beneficence.

The Father has planned well for the future of his material
children. They started in the dirt, in the corners of the universes,
not much different from the bacteria except for their ability to
someday know him. And this spark, this infinitesimally small
spark that he bestows on you, he will carefully husband until it
grows to a precious flickering flame, first yellow, then blue, then
white-hot—a torch, a jet, a cutting tool, a welding tool, a light
that illuminates lives, worlds, and universes, a searing white bril-
liance indistinguishable from his own, for it is him, of him, part
of him, an extension and expression of his love and desire to
share himself freely.

41

---

[1]  *The Urantia Book* teaches that on very rare occasions, an inhabited planet can
fall into tragedy as a result of rebellion in the celestial hierarchy that oversees
that world. Our planet, Urantia, is one of these unfortunate few. (See "Lucifer
Rebellion" in the glossary.)

[2]  "Mystery Monitor" is another term used for "indwelling spirit."

## THIS INDWELLING SPIRIT ("THOUGHT ADJUSTER") IS YOUR DIVINE PILOT

The Father fragment, your Thought Adjuster,[1] exists to provide a bridge between God and each person. In numerous places in *The Urantia Book,* the Adjuster is also called the Mystery Monitor, for it is also by this mechanism that the Father knows for himself what goes on in creation. Adjusters do not have personality. To do so, by definition, would be intrusive upon the human development of character.

The Adjuster's service is spent in turning the coarse into fine, in capitalizing on the best available method to shine light into the dark corners. The Adjuster is a great card player. He can make a hand out of practically anything. You provide him with the cards. He makes the best out of what he has. The Adjuster is at the far end of the road to perfection; therefore, it should be easy for him to entice you to follow the most productive path. But the fact is, few humans are listening.

Communication with the Father through the Adjuster is not what you think it will be. It will not be in a form that you will immediately recognize except in the feelings that it evokes in your human heart. The instantaneous response of your developing soul

---

The Adjuster is an absolute essence of an infinite being imprisoned within the mind of a finite creature which, depending on the choosing of such a mortal, can eventually consummate this temporary union of God and man and veritably actualize a new order of being for unending universe service. The Adjuster is the divine universe reality which factualizes the truth that God is man's Father. The Adjuster is man's infallible cosmic compass, always and unerringly pointing the soul Godward.

—*The Urantia Book,* pp. 1176–77

and the Father fragment is your guide, your compass. My teaching and the activities of this group meeting here—that's all frosting. The Adjuster is the compass. It always points north.

---

[1] The Thought Adjuster (also "Father fragment" or "Mystery Monitor") is further defined in this chapter and in the glossary. It is a technical term for the infinite spark of God within each person.

# THE INDWELLING SPIRIT ELEVATES
# THE QUALITY OF YOUR THOUGHTS

There are numerous references within the text of *The Urantia Book* to the deficiencies of your earthly languages in conveying accurate information about spiritual phenomena, spiritual personalities, and spiritual developments. When we first sought to identify a useful term to encapsulate the functions performed by the Father fragments in each of you, we faced a problem because of the unpredictable vagaries of your languages. We originally proposed, for example, to describe the Thought Adjusters as "Spiritual Receptivity Activators," which sounded altogether too mechanical. The term "Catalysts of Spiritual Progression" was proposed, but sounded too chemical.

We liked the phrase "spirit-led," which, in your society, is generally construed as a helpful description, but when we attempted to convey the notion of "led in thought," the connotation of that suggestion was seen to be negative. Even now, certain people automatically resent the implications of the term "Thought Adjuster."

The divine spirit makes contact with mortal man, not by feelings or emotions, but in the realm of the highest and most spiritualized thinking. It is your *thoughts*, not your feelings, that lead you Godward. The divine nature may be perceived only with the eyes of the mind. But the mind that really discerns God, hears the indwelling Adjuster, is the pure mind. "Without holiness no man may see the Lord." All such inner and spiritual communion is termed spiritual insight. Such religious experiences result from the impress made upon the mind of man by the combined operations of the Adjuster and the Spirit of Truth as they function amid and upon the ideas, ideals, insights, and spirit strivings of the evolving sons of God.

— *The Urantia Book*, pp. 1104–5

This created a quandary. In addition, because we sensed that people were largely uninterested in reference terms that emphasized the majesty and the only barely understandable miraculous qualities of this function of the Father, we only occasionally refer to Thought Adjusters by a term we prefer, "Mystery Monitors."

But even the term "Monitor" does not accurately convey the prime function of the Thought Adjusters, which is to elevate the quality of the spiritual component potential in your thoughts, when you have them. It is not required that the subject matter of your thoughts or the reaction to them be new or unknown; it is only necessary that you see with new perspective, that you approach even the same tired subject matter with new receptivity, with a fresh and spontaneous potential.

In that situation there is a thought, and the Adjuster—from natural talent and long-standing familiarity with the human of the indwelling—is uniquely suited to draw out the spiritual component, which, after all, is the only part of any value whatsoever to the heavenly Father. But for these things to be done, there must first be a thought.

The Adjusters cannot and will not place thoughts in your head. They do not trick you into seeing things or imagining things; they do not plant notions. They are totally reliant on you to make the first move. Until there is motion, the Adjusters can do nothing but wait.

# THE INDWELLING SPIRIT MAKES GOD INTIMATELY AVAILABLE TO ALL

The Father has not abandoned this world to perpetual spiritual poverty. Even if the Father were to recall all the ministering celestial entities who presently interact with the God-knowing and God-rejecting mortals on your world, only the *speed* of developments would be affected. This is so because the Father's direct participation in the life of each and every mortal, through the mechanism of the Adjuster, is the bedrock, the foundation, of all spiritual knowledge and progress.

The contribution of special instruction teams such as ours is minor in comparison with the breadth and scope of the Adjuster indwelling. For all our work, our result is poor. There have been defections and rebellions from within our ranks, but there has never been a failure by an Adjuster. Failure is impossible, by definition, for the Adjuster is a detached part of God himself, indwelling you. You have but to express an intent to better yourself, and the Adjuster will have already acted upon that thought—while it was being formed. The Adjuster has acted before we are even aware that an opportunity has dawned.

Our role—celestials, seraphim, and other ministering personalities—is limited to two areas of progress: overt, public declarations

*Unless a divine lover lived in man, he could not unselfishly and spiritually love. Unless an interpreter lived in the mind, man could not truly realize the unity of the universe. Unless an evaluator dwelt with man, he could not possibly appraise moral values and recognize spiritual meanings. And this lover hails from the very source of infinite love; this interpreter is a part of Universal Unity; this evaluator is the child of the Center and Source of all absolute values of divine and eternal reality.*

— *The Urantia Book,* p. 2094

of spiritual hunger; and personalized progress guidance. The ministry of the Father through the Adjuster, however, is in place *for every human*. It is not even a matter of choice for the human. God is reaching out, as he always has, making himself immediately and intimately available in the life of every conscious person.

In order to interrupt God's ministry, the human must resort to personality extinction,[1] so profound is the Father's commitment to his children. He will never abandon you, no matter how many times you may reject him. We look upon this relationship, this dedication, this perfection, with wonder, for it is unfailing in its application. The Father has blanketed creation with his personal ministry. We are in awe of the universal presence of the Father. Wherever we are asked to go, when we take up our duties, we find that he has already been there, many times.

For these, and all other good and sound reasons, we ask you to fear not. Go forward bravely, secure in the knowledge and comfort of the Father's love. Never forget that just as he loves and comforts you, so does he love and comfort each person you meet. That puts another face on things, and makes it difficult to dislike or reject your brothers and sisters, for the God fragment in each of them is inseparable, just as it is in you. Wherefore we ask that you love one another.

Do not fear your companions. Begin building the connections between people, linking up the weak with the strong, until all are surrounded with the totality and presence of the Father's ministry.

---

[1] Personality extinction is defined in *The Urantia Book* as death without the possibility of an afterlife resurrection.

# GOD IS NEVER ABSENT FROM HIS POST

There stands between you and the Father a vast space of knowledge—one that can be bridged only by daily prayer and involvement with the indwelling Adjuster and all the other spiritual help available to you. We work from without, and the indwelling Adjuster works within. He is the one to connect you immediately with our Father. If you have concerns, take them to the Adjuster, who is the Father in you. He will hear your petition.

Always does the Father listen to his children. The answer may not be immediately forthcoming, but it will come nonetheless. Those who are diligent in their prayer life will find the rewards great, for our Father is generous in his support of love and nourishes his child with all things on a spiritual level. Nothing is wanting and he will always be there—God is never absent from his post. While you humans have forgotten him in your daily life, he never forgets you. After your day is over, think of all the ways during the day he was with you and you were not even aware of it—in the smile of another or in the kindness of a stranger. Our Father makes time for us; let us make time for him.

> Do not allow the magnitude of the infinity, the immensity of the eternity, and the grandeur and glory of the matchless character of God to overawe, stagger, or discourage you; for the Father is not very far from any one of you; he dwells within you, and in him do we all literally move, actually live, and veritably have our being.
> —*The Urantia Book*, p. 139

# THE SPIRIT'S REALM IS THE PRESENT MOMENT

We are all family—you and I, and those unknown to us. But in order for us to know the Father intimately, we must forgo our near-obsession with planning for the future, which may never arrive. It is not how well we have planned for some distant future that counts in heaven; it is the history that we accumulate living moment by moment in the present, where the Father fragment can communicate with us. The Adjuster cannot inhabit the future. He can arrive only when we arrive. He cannot live in the past; it is a closed book. The Adjuster's realm is in the present, the right now, this moment, in the thoughts and the urgings, in the deeds performed with his leadings. If you are to make progress and you wish to know the Father, you must know him right now. This is the limitation on material life creatures. You are not time-fluid. Those moments you spend living in the future and living in the past are lost forever. Pay attention to today; the future will take care of itself. It is in God's hands. You can bring no great influence to bear anyway.

The Adjuster can act only at the knife's edge, where it is risky, where things are not under control, where the sparks are likely to strike. If you back off into the realm of safety and failed communications, then you immediately raise barriers not only between yourself and your opposite number, but also between the Adjuster resident in

The divine presence cannot, however, be discovered anywhere in nature or even in the lives of God-knowing mortals so fully and so certainly as in your attempted communion with the indwelling Mystery Monitor, the Paradise Thought Adjuster. What a mistake to dream of God far off in the skies when the spirit of the Universal Father lives within your own mind!

—*The Urantia Book*, p. 64

you and the Adjuster fragment that inhabits the other party. Therefore, we have exhorted you to take chances, to speak candidly, honestly, forthrightly, and genuinely with those you encounter, for that is where the Adjuster will have his way. You can feel his pull. It is like a vortex; you are drawn up and forward and out. It is exhilarating. You must take the chance; we think you will like the experience. But you must live in the present in order to do so. When you live in the present, you live in the realm that God inhabits.

# FOLLOW THE SPIRIT'S LEADING—
## AIM HIGH

I cannot really instruct you on how to more closely attune your-self to your Adjuster's leading. Response to that leading does not lend itself to mechanistic descriptions and terminology; it is, rather, a relationship. Each of you has a relationship with God, who remains unseen, who speaks not to you in words that you understand. The heavenly Father reveals himself by methods that suit his purposes, yet his influence colors your every waking moment and fills your dreams with desire for attainment of perfection.

Each person on this planet is on a unique path following the blazes laid down by his or her Adjuster far ahead, out of sight. We, the members of your instruction team, your humble teachers, encourage you to follow the Adjuster's leading, to aim high.

All humans of the material worlds are faced with two apparently irreconcilable demands. Those who know God and who would live according to his will are faced with the competing and conflicting demands of the material world. Compromise with the material world is inevitable, yet compromise on the path of spiritual progress is impossible.

You are growing, and when you find yourselves in compromising situations, remember that you are becoming increasingly spiritual creatures and you are using this material life experience to become

M ind is your ship, the Adjuster is your pilot, the human will is captain. The master of the mortal vessel should have the wisdom to trust the divine pilot to guide the ascending soul into the. . . harbors of eternal survival. . . . With your consent, this faithful pilot will safely carry you across the barriers of time and the handicaps of space to the very source of the divine mind and on beyond, even to the Paradise Father.

—*The Urantia Book*, p. 1217

*The Indwelling Spirit: Infinite Gift of Love*

progressively spiritual. It is not the other way around. You are not growing in spiritual strength to become more successful in any material sense.

This material life experience is denied to most of the orders of creatures in the Universe. You are those selected by the great God to see the entire scope of creation, from the lowest to the most infinite. The fact of material life inevitably creates some severe restrictions upon your time, yet, particularly in your modern society, we feel that sufficient time exists to devote meaningful units of daily organizational time to spiritual growth and honest, direct, loving service to your fellow humans as the opportunity arises. We say to you that you need not go to any particular place to be about the Father's work. There is work to be done here in this room. How much more there is beyond the door.

# CHAPTER 4

# STILLNESS: THE TECHNIQUE OF CENTERING

# STILLNESS OPENS YOU TO THE VITALITY OF GOD

*I*t is simply impossible to hear the voice of God amid the chatter and drivel of modern society's daily life. These distractions drown out the faint beginnings of spiritual awareness. But for all things a beginning is necessary. Therefore we ask you to try, on a daily basis, to compose yourself in stillness. The way to begin is to clear your mind. Don't think about anything. Don't think about *not* thinking. We do not prescribe that in practicing stillness you attempt to stop your thoughts. Stillness, like life in general, is about keeping your mind on the most important thing. It is not necessary to root out all your thoughts. Simply let them pass through. They are only bit players on the scene anyway. Just allow your mind to come to rest naturally and you will find a stillness that has great vitality. In that stillness you will be able to discern the vitality of God, even in what you thought were the empty spaces. Those who can find meaning in the empty spaces are truly on the right path.

---

*B*ut the greatest of all methods of problem solving I have learned from Jesus, your Master. I refer to that which he so consistently practices, and which he has so faithfully taught you, the isolation of worshipful meditation. In this habit of Jesus' going off so frequently by himself to commune with the Father in heaven is to be found the technique, not only of gathering strength and wisdom for the ordinary conflicts of living, but also of appropriating the energy for the solution of the higher problems of a moral and spiritual nature. But even correct methods of solving problems will not compensate for inherent defects of personality or atone for the absence of the hunger and thirst for true righteousness.[1]

—*The Urantia Book,* p. 1774

---

Your stillness practice is a matter of discipline. You will find that as your practice progresses, it will become a respite from the abuses of daily living; if for no other reason, this quiet time itself could be one of the most valuable features of your day.

---

[1] This and the next three *Urantia Book* quotes are excerpted from the observations of a Greek philosopher from Alexandria named Rodan, a contemporary of Jesus who became a believer in his teachings.

The method we recommend for increasing your understanding of perfection is regular stillness practice. By quieting yourself and making time available for the heavenly Father in your busy schedule, you are allowing, even soliciting, Thought Adjuster tuning. The sad fact is that for most humans on your planet, the Adjuster is capable of acting only during periods of great distress or during the cessation of conscious human activity, specifically sleep. And, although a great deal of your earthly life is taken up in sleep and rest periods, this is not the ideal situation for the Adjuster's work. There is no substitute for the conscious embrace of the heavenly Father's love and beneficence. None of you would go your entire lives without an expression of love and compassion and respect toward your earth parents, and yet many people on your planet would treat their heavenly Father in just such a manner. Worse yet, this phenomenon is pervasive in the most technologically and materially advanced societies on your planet.

Jesus has taught us that God lives in man; then how can we induce man to release these soul-bound powers of divinity and infinity? How shall we induce men to let go of God that he may bring forth to the refreshment of our own souls while in transit outward and then to serve the purpose of enlightening, uplifting, and blessing countless other souls? How best can I awaken these latent powers for good which lie dormant in your souls? One thing I am sure of: Emotional excitement is not the ideal spiritual stimulus. Excitement does not augment energy; it rather exhausts the powers of both mind and body. Whence then comes the energy to do these great things? Look to your Master. Even now he is out in the hills taking in power while we are here giving out energy.

—*The Urantia Book*, p. 1777

You will greatly benefit from this time spent with the heavenly Father. You would even benefit if all you ever did was stop the human chatter for some period of time; this fact has been known to many cultures and for many centuries. What we ask is that you consciously make time for God. Make yourself available to hear his voice, to feel the pull of his magnetism, to feel the flow of his love and to attune yourself, however imperceptibly, closer to his plan, which only a few personalities in all the universes can comprehend.

# REGULARITY OF STILLNESS PRACTICE IS ESSENTIAL

*I*n practicing stillness, availability for the heavenly Father is what is desired. Next, regularity is desired. By this we do not mean any specific frame of mind or attitude or mindset, nor do we mean any particular time of day. By regularity we mean only a good and faithful ordinary attempt to practice on a regular basis. Because you are just beginning, we feel that modesty is an appropriate goal. Ten minutes are asked, twenty minutes in the farther reaches.

Our experience in observing people in your society in this period of history is that substantially more than twenty minutes is likely to be unproductive. This does not mean that to practice longer will be offensive in any way. It is just that statistically it has

> *I* am deeply impressed with the custom of Jesus in going apart by himself to engage in these seasons of solitary survey of the problems of living; to seek for new stores of wisdom and energy for meeting the manifold demands of social service; to quicken and deepen the supreme purpose of living by actually subjecting the total personality to the consciousness of contacting with divinity; to grasp for possession of new and better methods of adjusting oneself to the ever-changing situations of living existence; to effect those vital reconstructions and readjustments of one's personal attitudes which are so essential to enhanced insight into everything worthwhile and real; and to do all of this with an eye single to the glory of God—to breathe in sincerity your Master's favorite prayer, "Not my will, but yours, be done."
>
> The relaxation of worship, or spiritual communion as practiced by the Master, relieves tension, removes conflicts, and mightily augments the total resources of the personality. And all this philosophy, plus the gospel of the kingdom, constitutes the new religion as I understand it.
>
> —*The Urantia Book,* p. 1774

been shown to be unproductive. We have experimented with this at great length.

Do not trouble yourself over the amount of time. The heavenly Father is always willing to communicate. It is not necessary that you say any particular thing or think any particular thought or pursue any particular notion. Your simple availability is how it all begins.

# CORRECT PHYSICAL POSTURE IS HELPFUL

There are a few parameters of psychological and physiological character that have effects upon stillness practice. We prefer, for example, that you not attempt stillness practice when you are near the extreme reaches of physical effort. At such a time your body needs sleep—rest at the very least. The Father will not interfere with that.

Neither should you take a large dose of stimulating drugs, such as tea or coffee. That situation would be equally unproductive—in fact, a polar opposite to stillness of mind. Nor would it be especially effective if a person were in a greatly agitated emotional state, although we will say that stillness is generally the proper remedy for agitation and should work to swiftly bring you back into balance with your normal self. This is not equal to communication with the heavenly Father, however.

I will say that the ideal would be an attitude of relaxed alertness. We have many times remarked that stillness practice must be conscious. In simple fashion, it is easy to figure out that certain body positions are more productive of relaxed alertness: In a general sense, body positions that tend to interrupt the flow of physical energy also tend to produce impairment of the flow of energy. This will cause a diminution of the available body energy, with a negative

The secret...is wrapped up in spiritual communion, in worship. From the human standpoint it is a question of combined meditation and relaxation. Meditation makes the contact of mind with spirit; relaxation determines the capacity for spiritual receptivity. And this interchange of strength for weakness, courage for fear, the will of God for the mind of self, constitutes worship.

—*The Urantia Book*, p. 1777

effect upon relaxed alertness. We have no preference for one body posture, but I would say a person should maintain an erect position, relaxed, with the limbs in some natural resting position—not twisted, tied, or knotted in any particular mystical fashion.

# Don't Let the Ego Trivialize Your Stillness

By design, you are intended to be thinking creatures. Your thoughts are one of your chief products. You might even say that thoughts are part of the currency of the universe. It is the interchange of ideas expressed as thoughts that provides the way for people to gain experience, to gain understanding, to gain a modicum of wisdom without having to endure the necessity of individual discovery of every facet of the universe. That is why I can say that thoughts are part of the currency of the universe.

One of the design flaws of the ego is that it attempts to organize things for which it is unfit. The ego tries to extend its authority into areas of the personality where it is not properly designed for preeminence. For example, the human ego will attempt to organize and thereby inescapably trivialize spiritual experience. It will seek to categorize and pair off in polar opposites those experiences that might otherwise be quite productive. The ego does this any time you focus attention and is naturally intended to function in this manner. Rather than focusing your attention upon any particular thought, which the ego naturally interprets as needing some organization, allow that thought to float past and off the stage. Do not vex yourself over your thoughts.

We recommend that you attempt stillness practice for ten, or at most twenty, minutes at a time. If you find that you are burdened

> Jesus taught his followers that, when they had made their prayers to the Father, they should remain for a time in silent receptivity to afford the indwelling spirit the better opportunity to speak to the listening soul. The spirit of the Father speaks best to man when the human mind is in an attitude of true worship.
>
> —*The Urantia Book*, p. 1641

with extraneous thoughts during your stillness practice at a regular time each day, experiment with the time frame in which you practice your stillness. You might find a certain time of day more conducive to your practice.

# DECREASE THE TIME DEMANDS ON YOUR DAILY LIVES

*I*n your material careers, you must learn to say no to many temptations. When work demands become unreasonable, you must likewise learn to say no to them also, else you will be ensuring a repeat demand on the morrow. Your North American civilization has progressed so far, in so short a time, chiefly on the contributions of its casualties and not on the abilities of the successful. This unrestrained consumption of the participants, typically labeled social Darwinism, is better named by its more virulent critics: dog-eat-dog. This is no path for aspiring or enlightened seekers to continue to tread. While it is useless to rewrite history, it is equally useless to repeat it.

We say to you that it is fundamentally inconsistent with the true search for the Father to tolerate or contribute to the exploitation of the people—and this is as true where you yourselves are exploited as it is of your brothers and sisters. There are only so many days allotted to each, and it is piracy to take away all of the people's time.

*T*he great challenge to modern man is to achieve better communication with the divine Monitor that dwells within the human mind. Man's greatest adventure in the flesh consists in the well-balanced and sane effort to advance the borders of self-consciousness out through the dim realms of embryonic soul-consciousness in a wholehearted effort to reach the borderland of spirit-consciousness—contact with the divine presence. Such an experience constitutes God-consciousness—an experience mightily confirmative of the pre-existent truth of the religious experience of knowing God. Such spirit-consciousness is the equivalent of the knowledge of the actuality of sonship with God. Otherwise, the assurance of sonship is the experience of faith.

—*The Urantia Book*, p. 2097

We have requested that you make time in your lives for the Father; only ten minutes of daily silent prayer has been asked. Yet it can easily be seen that, even so, there seems to be insufficient time that you make available in your lives to engage in the Father's good work, if such an opportunity were to present itself.

So we ask that in order to prepare for service activity, you begin to decrease the time demands on your daily lives. This will not be easy for any of you, but it must be done. If we never exchanged another word, by letter or in a meeting, a decrease in your time commitments would still be necessary. This development is yet in the future for your world, especially for your modern societies, but it will come to pass.

There is much to learn and you all have very busy lives. It is good that you are taking time out each day to attach yourselves to the spiritual realms. You cannot do anything effectively without the Father's help. You may think you can, but in the long run, you could finish things much more smoothly with his help.

# CHAPTER 5

# THE MEANING AND PURPOSE OF STILLNESS PRACTICE

# FINDING THE DOOR TO STILLNESS TAKES EFFORT

*I*t is not always comfortable to be alone with God. The experience is usually full of intrusive thoughts. You wonder where to put your feet, how you should hold your mouth, whether you should think certain things or not think certain things. It is difficult to instruct people in what they should do. I will tell you frankly that regularity is more important than success.

The stillness practice means going into the quiet place in yourself. Many people find this place to be theoretical. They agree that it must be somewhere, but all the doors look the same. For most people, successful stillness practice means marking the door. Once you move away from the door you are subject to all of the other factors of life: the times you are excited, the times you are relaxed, the times when the pressures of daily life catch up, the times they are discharged, the times you worry about the things that have yet to pass and those that already have. Eventually, you find the door with the mark on it, you straighten your back and open it—but you see nothing. This is frustrating to most people.

I think the best description of it is this: standing on the bow of a large ship so far above the water and so far projected forward that

> *O*n every mountaintop of intellectual thought are to be found relaxation for the mind, strength for the soul, and communion for the spirit. From such vantage points of high living, man is able to transcend the material irritations of the lower levels of thinking—worry, jealousy, envy, revenge, and the pride of immature personality. These high-climbing souls deliver themselves from a multitude of the crosscurrent conflicts of the trifles of living, thus becoming free to attain consciousness of the higher currents of spirit concept and celestial communication.
>
> —*The Urantia Book*, p. 1778

even the ship's prow, cutting through the waves, makes no sound that reaches the listener. You look out into the fog, all your senses keen, and there is simply no information. No thoughts, no vision, no smells, no sounds, no feelings; and yet you are surrounded with concern and love and guidance.

# STILLNESS IS NOT A QUICK FIX

*O*ur God is a good God. Friendly. True. His love is limited only by justice and, even then, all his other qualities seep through. Our God, as we understand him, is primarily love to be shared equally among all his children. By consciously stilling yourself, you make it possible for the indwelling Thought Adjuster to go about the Father's work in a new atmosphere, in an arena not available otherwise.

We ask that you view our request for ten minutes of daily silent prayer as a minimum in terms of both occasion and length of attention. We ask you to consider stillness practice twice a day for the same ten-minute period. You are welcome to exceed this. At the moment, I think we can safely say that this will not take over your daily life. None of you are in jeopardy of devoting your entire earthly life to the Father's service. It is early yet and the road in front of us is long. We make a modest request.

All of you are in the habit of looking for results immediately, but only those results that take time to achieve are really worth

*W*hen these experiences are frequently repeated, they crystallize into habits, strength-giving and worshipful habits, and such habits eventually formulate themselves into a spiritual character, and such a character is finally recognized by one's fellows as a *mature personality*. These practices are difficult and time-consuming at first, but when they become habitual, they are at once restful and time-saving. The more complex society becomes, and the more the lures of civilization multiply, the more urgent will become the necessity for God-knowing individuals to form such protective habitual practices designed to conserve and augment their spiritual energies.

—*The Urantia Book*, p. 1777

pursuing. You should deduce now from your reading of *The Urantia Book* that there are no quick fixes. Therefore, we encourage you to apply yourselves with an increasing appreciation of the amount of time required to effect any substantial change. We think that the indications of this truth are all around you, yet many humans fail to perceive this lesson. Everything in *The Urantia Book* counsels evolution, not revolution; transition, not sweeping change.

# SIMPLE AVAILABILITY IS THE KEY

*T*ranscendental Meditation and similar techniques of meditation are recommended, except to the extent that they lead to obliteration of consciousness. An absolute requirement of stillness practice, as taught in this ministry, is consciousness. You must be conscious. Therefore, we attempt to discourage people from becoming entangled in elaborate schemes of self-projection or identification with natural phenomena or celestial bodies in the astronomic sky. Where you are, who you are, is always good enough for God. You need not remake yourself. God loves you anyway.

God's communication with you is not conveyed with human words—certainly not in the English language nor in any language we recognize. God's communication is spirit to spirit, spark to spark, forehead to forehead, palm to palm. You are becoming progressively spiritualized. As you make progress, your communication with the Father is more complete, has more depth, more breadth. You are increasing your contact area at the point of intersection, with results that I will leave to your imagination. That, too, is part of the experience.

It is not necessary to think certain thoughts or to listen to certain sounds or even to hope to identify and repeat certain feelings that are naturally spawned by the active communication, person to person, with the heavenly Father. It is enough for you to earn all the necessary stripes simply by making yourself available. That is

> *M*ortals live in God, and so God has willed to live in mortals. As men trust themselves to him, so has he—and first—trusted a part of himself to be with men; has consented to live in men and to indwell men subject to the human will.
>
> —*The Urantia Book*, p. 1221

the most important part. Make yourself available to God. What you do or don't do or try to do in addition to that simple fact of availability is trivial. I can say with absolute authority that God appreciates you. He is waiting to share himself. He is ever polite in his manners. By making yourself available, you invite him to enter your life.

Through the normal ups and downs of life, which vary from hour to hour, great variety is experienced in the type and tenacity of connection available with the heavenly Father. It is meant to be so. To the extent that you identify a practical and productive place where you go to make yourself available to the Father, we encourage you to use it, yet we will say that it is not exclusive. The Father is always there. The only limitations on your communication with him are those you impose upon yourselves. This doesn't have to be a dreary exercise. There is no reason why communication with the Father should not be lighthearted and happy. Availability is the key.

# STILLNESS BUILDS A NEW LIFE
## BEYOND EGO'S CONTROL

The heavenly Father does not need stillness practice. You do. You are the ones who will benefit. God is already perfect. You are not expected to see immediate results from stillness practice. You are not expected to see significance in this conduct. You are expected to calm your animal minds by controlling the runaway ego, which seeks to organize areas in which the ego does not belong. You have stray thoughts because your ego attempts to organize your adoration of the heavenly Father.

The human ego is an adaptive tool that efficiently serves the demands of the material life, but it has nothing whatever to do with the spirit life. Each time you do stillness practice you build spirit life, whether you know it or not, by creating a new life not under the control of the human ego.

Countless generations of wise people on your planet have engaged in techniques similar to these and found good results. This is not new. It is not some trick whereby we enslave you without your knowledge. You're free to participate or not to participate. The only thing that will change is you.

By the old way you seek to suppress, obey, and conform to the rules of living; by the new way you are first *transformed* by the Spirit of Truth and thereby strengthened in your inner soul by the constant spiritual renewing of your mind, and so are you endowed with the power of the certain and joyous performance of the gracious, acceptable, and perfect will of God.

—Jesus speaking at an evening conference with the Apostles,
*The Urantia Book,* p. 1609

# THE RIVER OF LOVE FLOWS
# OVER ALL, REGARDLESS

You have asked whether alcohol, or marijuana or some other drug used for relaxation, interferes with or somehow hinders a person's ability to achieve stillness or receive spiritual sustenance.

Considering liquor as a type of drug, the effect of all drugs upon the human is to render the human more or less senseless. You're not damaging the heavenly Father and the effect on yourself is only temporary, but your ability to recognize the results of stillness is reduced. The short answer is: The process continues unabated. The time spent is the most important thing. Functionally there is little difference between stillness approached from an attitude of natural excitement or natural depression or unnatural sedation. The river of love flows over all. It is unstoppable. Your ability to perceive it is perhaps diminished. The Father prefers that when humans report for duty, they bring with them their full complement of wits, but the most important thing is that they are on duty.

And, Flavius, I declare that in the coming kingdom they shall no longer teach, 'Do not worship this and do not worship that'; no longer shall they concern themselves with commands to refrain from this and take care not to do that, but rather shall all be concerned with one supreme duty. And this duty of man is expressed in two great privileges: sincere worship of the infinite Creator, the Paradise Father, and loving service bestowed upon one's fellow men. If you love your neighbor as you love yourself, you really know that you are a son of God.

—Jesus speaking to Flavius, the Greek Jew, *The Urantia Book,* p. 1600

# STILLNESS CAN DISSOLVE PROBLEMS

*I* urge you to practice your own stillness. You will not regret it. We realize there are times when your lives are very active and you truly do not have time, but many of you are engaged in activities that, from the spiritual perspective, are a waste of time. While you need your recreation, instead of wasting time, you could be spending time with your heavenly Father. All that we have asked you to do is spend ten to twenty minutes each day, twice a day if you are able.

How much lighter would be the burden you carry if you would only find this time. The solutions you seek to daily problems, the struggles you encounter, the relationships that seem strained will all be resolved, and in their place you will find peace, contentment, and a peace of mind that comes only from the Father. The inner Adjuster helps whenever you are attuned; he stands alert to help you in whatever way you allow him to do so.

So take that time. If you have that special place, wherever it is, find yourself in it and seek your Father's presence. All of us have things we look back upon and wish we could have done differently, but we cannot go back—we can only look to the future with hope and with our dreams of things that remain to be fulfilled. We can have a new beginning now.

*P*ersonal, spiritual religious experience is an efficient solvent for most mortal difficulties; it is an effective sorter, evaluator, and adjuster of all human problems. Religion does not remove or destroy human troubles, but it does dissolve, absorb, illuminate, and transcend them. True religion unifies the personality for effective adjustment to all mortal requirements.

—*The Urantia Book,* p. 2093

# THE INDWELLING SPIRIT IS NOTHING BUT SPONTANEOUS

You have asked how you can measure success in stillness, how you can know if you've made the connection with the Father, so that you can attain it again. I will say this, and I do not mean it to be harsh. To try to recapture or repeat an experience is generally a bad idea. The ego will overtake the repeated experience and trivialize it for you.

There is no way to know whether a person is making fast progress or slow progress or progress on a tangent. Even if I were to counsel you, it would be worthless. What you seek is in the realm of the Adjuster. The Adjuster is your guide. The lessons presented may or may not prove productive. But I think I can guarantee that the method by which the Adjuster operates will always contain an element of surprise. The Adjuster, by nature, can be nothing but spontaneous.

This is a discomforting situation for the human and explains, in large measure, why people have created bureaucracies to administer the relationship between man and God. There is no such thing as comfortable spiritual growth. It is always disturbing. It is always provocative. But the result is usually happy.

Faith is the inspiration of the spiritized creative imagination.
—*The Urantia Book,* p. 1459

# HEAVEN DOES NOT SPEAK—IT ACTS

*I* prescribe regular practice first. Everything will settle down. It takes time. I do not mean this to sound harsh, but those who will not take the time will find the going very difficult indeed. It is human skill to calm yourself. It is a human reaction to fill up all the empty spaces with chatter. It is merely your soul desiring company. You can get control of it, but you will not control yourself by making war upon yourself. Sit quietly and wait. Peace will come. Heaven speaks not a word but acts always. God cannot be limited by an Earth language. He will communicate to you spirit-to-spirit. There is no other way. That communication takes place by the rules of the universe with which you are only rudely acquainted. It is fine for you to speak to him in words. What comes back to you is love.

*B*ut your unsteady and rapidly shifting mental attitudes often result in thwarting the plans and interrupting the work of the Adjusters. Their work is not only interfered with by the innate natures of the mortal races, but this ministry is also greatly retarded by your own preconceived opinions, settled ideas, and long-standing prejudices. Because of these handicaps, many times only their unfinished creations emerge into consciousness, and confusion of concept is inevitable. Therefore, in scrutinizing mental situations, safety lies only in the prompt recognition of each and every thought and experience for just what it actually and fundamentally is, disregarding entirely what it might have been.

—*The Urantia Book*, p. 1199

# THE INDWELLING SPIRIT IS THE SOURCE OF OUR DESIRE FOR PERFECTION

*N*ow that we have some grasp of the meaning and the purpose of stillness practice, I would like to say a few words about the beneficial effects of regular stillness practice as an enticement to those of you who are not practicing regularly or are not practicing as often as you would like.

We could refer to stillness practice as Adjuster tuning. It's like tuning a radio to God's station. God doesn't always come through loud and clear. It depends on the quality of the tuner. But with regular practice, it is easier to find the mark. Before long, it becomes an increasingly worthwhile experience.

*The Urantia Book* teaches that the presence of the Thought Adjuster is the source of all human desire for perfection, and I think that this is so. Any savage in the forest can distinguish between the relative degrees of utility offered by a stone ax head and a steel ax head, or between overripe food and ripe food. At the other end of the scale, it's also possible to distinguish between a service that is provided for immediate selfish gain and one provided out of love and respect for the heavenly Father's desires. The presence of the Adjuster makes all these things possible in a human, for even though it is theoretically possible for animals to

> *T*he work of the Thought Adjuster constitutes the explanation of the translation of man's primitive and evolutionary sense of duty into that higher and more certain faith in the eternal realities of revelation. There must be perfection hunger in man's heart to insure capacity for comprehending the faith paths to supreme attainment. If any man chooses to do the divine will, he shall know the way of truth.
>
> —*The Urantia Book,* p. 1118

distinguish between good and better, they have no need to. It is not a gratifying distinction for them, and this is what, in part, sets humans apart from the animals—the gratifying knowledge of the ability to discern the more perfect.

This is only part of the gift that the Father has bestowed upon you, for an increasing awareness of the beauty of perfection is its own reward. This awareness provides incentive for human conduct with or without any connection to any community, with or without any material reward, with or without any conscious thought whatever. And so I can say with confidence that when you tune yourself to God's voice, you will receive direct and palpable rewards. You will know that they are spiritual rewards because no other person's approval or pronouncement is necessary for you to substantiate the experience.

# STILLNESS IS IMPLICIT IN THE TEACHINGS OF THE URANTIA BOOK

*The Urantia Book* is a revelatory text. It both implicitly and explicitly counsels direct relationship with the Father, yet it was thought that to include prescriptions of mechanisms already widely known by several cultures on your planet would cause the book to be received and analyzed as a manual and not as a text.

At the time *The Urantia Book* was compiled and published, this planet was isolated. Under a special dispensation, the work continued on the book. It was decided ultimately to go to publication in the hope of providing a cornerstone that would be a valuable reference point for all persons and all cultures. Therefore, no mechanisms other than the recitation of the techniques used by Jesus of Nazareth were included in the text.

*The Urantia Book* is for all people. Many readers approach and use the book from an intellectual perspective only. Others find its lessons too profound and disturbing. Others find that it is just right. Everyone finds God—it is just a question of when. Individual instruction of humans on the planet has always gone forward on a case-by-case basis, and the Father's Adjuster ministry

*The* world needs more firsthand religion. Even Christianity—the best of the religions of the twentieth century—is not only a religion *about* Jesus, but it is so largely one which men experience secondhand. They take their religion wholly as handed down by their accepted religious teachers. What an awakening the world would experience if it could only see Jesus as he really lived on earth and know, firsthand, his life-giving teachings! Descriptive words of things beautiful cannot thrill like the sight thereof, neither can creedal words inspire men's souls like the experience of knowing the presence of God.

—*The Urantia Book*, p. 2083

has continued unimpeded for all time. But it was thought—and this is still accurate—that many techniques exist among the several religions of your planet that are very close to the stillness practice. It was believed that people would, in a natural fashion, discover those techniques and begin to apply them.

This has not happened to the extent we desired, but then, what has? And so when this ministry began, it was felt that rather than offering personal guidance, the correct thing to do, the most productive thing to do, would be to emphasize stillness as a technique for finding the Father individually and in group settings. We have had some success with this.

It is not important to understand how and why stillness works. It is only important to do it. Even if it rises to nothing more than a gesture of respect, it still works. That is all that is requested. You need do nothing more. But, of course, life can be much more rich, and the participation of the living spirit brings its own rewards. Therefore, we hammer and chisel and lever and sandbag people— daily, weekly, from within and without—with suggestions designed to reveal to them the feeling that comes from greater participation in the Father's creation. We encourage them to embrace more fully the life experience on the material planets and the feeling of love that flows vertically from the Father above and horizontally among the people.

# PART II

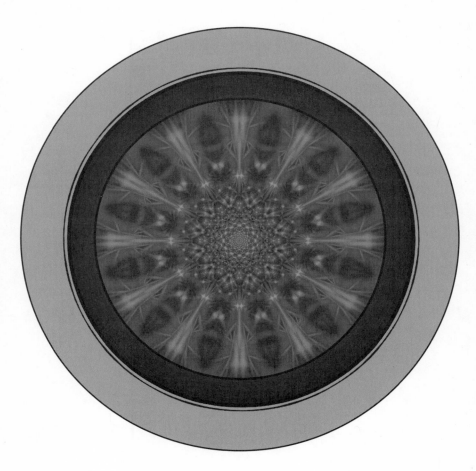

# LIVING THE
# GOD-CENTERED LIFE

# CHAPTER 6

# DISCERNING THE DIVINE WILL

# JESUS NEVER ERRED BECAUSE HE SOUGHT GOD'S WILL

*T*here is solace to be found in a personal relationship with the Father in heaven. It is good to know that we are not alone, is it not? We urge you all not to neglect precious time that you spend daily with the heavenly Father. There is no substitute for it. It is the bond that heals all wounds. Close and frequent communication with the heavenly Father is the secret of the Master's success. Though divine, he exercised fully human capabilities in his early and frequent communications; this led to the production of his sterling character and the kind of self-confidence that was unknown on the planet until his life revealed the Father's will.

The Master was never lured off the true path because he consciously, consistently, by his every thought and deed, dedicated himself to the will of the heavenly Father. He avoided consistently the trap of the extremes of the material life. He concerned himself only with the basics, divined the Father's will in each situation, and followed that course of action. Therefore, his faith was never shaken and he made no mistake.

There is a lesson in the Master's singlemindedness. When you are assailed by the events and circumstances of the material life, look within, seek the peace that exists for you—it is freely given to you—and request instruction in determining the ways that best serve the Father's will.

*J*esus brought to God, as a man of the realm, the greatest of all offerings: the consecration and dedication of his own will to the majestic service of doing the divine will. Jesus always and consistently interpreted religion wholly in terms of the Father's will.
—*The Urantia Book*, p. 2088

# THE FATHER'S WILL IS STRANGE AT FIRST

When first we begin to seek the Father's will for us, we step out into strange and unfamiliar territory. We are not used to seeking another's will, for we have been so used to seeking our own. And so it takes perseverance, as well as a strong, solid commitment. It takes daily seeking to strengthen this new purpose one has taken on.

Each time you seek the Father within, ask him for his guidance, accepting and appreciating his love and asking to know his will in your life. Each time you do this, it strengthens that connection with him who resides within each of us. It is not an easy task, but what comes easily is so often not of value. We would do your work for you if we could, but it must be a personal choice; it must be a wholehearted commitment from you to your Father who loves you. Open your hearts and find him, my dear ones; know that he is there. Embrace each new day filled with his light and end it the same, allowing him to bathe each experience with his love.

The will of God is the way of God, partnership with the choice of God in the face of any potential alternative. To do the will of God, therefore, is the progressive experience of becoming more and more like God, and God is the source and destiny of all that is good and beautiful and true. The will of man is the way of man, the sum and substance of that which the mortal chooses to be and do. Will is the deliberate choice of a self-conscious being which leads to decision-conduct based on intelligent reflection.

—*The Urantia Book*, p. 1431

# ALWAYS TURN TO THE FATHER FIRST

The Universe is designed so that those who have chosen the path to the Father may have every opportunity for growth and development. It is necessary at times to place before them challenges that require decisions that nurture the soul.

We watch urgently as one of you falters and then finds a firm footing on steady rock. It matters not that the footing was shaky at first. What does matter is the final outcome. Be patient with yourselves as we are patient with you. Only God knows how long it will take for you to acknowledge your own weaknesses and turn to him for support.

Some of you think you have the ability to tread the waters alone. Such is simply not the case. You must learn to rely upon the Father in all situations. Lean not to your own understanding, but call upon him while he is near. He will be ever vigilant in helping you.

Once you are finally aware of the reliability of your heavenly Father, you will turn to him first. There will be no need to spend even a moment in fear. Anxiety will pass you by and you will no longer be concerned about the future. Be not anxious about tomorrow. Sufficient is today and the troubles thereof. He is with you always.

Devote yourselves to your work, believing that both the Father and I know that you have need of all these things. Let me assure you, once and for all, that, if you dedicate your lives to the work of the kingdom, all your real needs shall be supplied. Seek the greater thing, and the lesser will be found therein; ask for the heavenly, and the earthly shall be included.

— Jesus to the twelve Apostles, *The Urantia Book*, p. 1823

# THE FATHER'S WILL ALWAYS ENTAILS SERVICE AND LOVE

*I* would like tonight to speak about doing the Father's will. Each of you feels a calling, an urge, a nudging to do something to use the abilities that God has granted you to further his will. You speak of the belief that these desires are nonexclusive, not limited to this group, but, indeed, are being felt throughout this planet, and I can confirm this. There is no "chosen" group, for, as you know, you are all God's children and God does not play favorites.

Many people do feel that something is afoot, but they can't put their finger on it. And, while your vision of the future may or may not be correct, a spiritual uplifting is, indeed, in progress and many are ready to hear the good news.

With so many people on this planet feeling the urge to reorient their priorities toward spiritual matters, be bold, step forth, provide them with an opportunity to discuss such things with you. You may be surprised at the reaction you get when you broach spiritual matters. Even those you think would be uninterested in such conversation may take up the topic with a vigor that will surprise you. Each of you will be a catalyst in this process.

This brings me back to the Father's will. Clearly, I cannot tell any person what the Father's will is for that person. It is an individual determination that you must make for yourself. I can say this, however: It entails a service to your brothers and sisters, an

*I* lived my life in the flesh to show how you can, through loving service, become God-revealing to your fellow men even as, by loving you and serving you, I have become God-revealing to you. I have lived among you as the Son of Man that you, and all other men, might know that you are all indeed the sons of God.

—Jesus' resurrection appearance in Jerusalem, *The Urantia Book,* p. 2053

assistance in spreading love to those you encounter. This power that lives within you is your guide. You are the captain and you must make the decision whether to follow this guide or not. But you can be assured that the path with the most love in it will not be far off the target.

To know the Father's will for your own self, seek the Father, converse with the Father, listen to the Father in your daily stillness meditations and practice. You have within you the most powerful piece of divinity that exists, and failing to consult with this guide is a mistake. You may speak with celestial teachers, you may speak with each other, and certainly all of that is well and good. But let none of it stand in the way of your stillness practice, for in the stillness are the answers.

# TAKE NOTE OF YOUR CHOICE: HIS WILL OR YOURS

*O*ne of you mentioned this evening that you are disappointed because you were given an internal nudge by your Adjuster and yet overrode it and asserted your own will above his. This is a common occurrence on a world such as yours, and yet it is our purpose to help you to recognize the times when your Adjuster does indeed connect with you. Upon waking and, hopefully, after having spent time within the stillness, we ask that you make a conscious commitment to turn your life over to your indwelling Adjuster: Open the eyes of your heart, if you will, and listen for his guidance.

When you recognize that you have been led—or nudged, if you prefer that term—we ask you to take note of it. Take note of the times when you hear and you choose the Father's will above your own; take note also of times when you hear and you assert your own will above that of the Father; and take note of the times when you hear and decide to assert your own will and then change your mind and decide to follow the Father. Whenever you take note of the direction that you have been given, you deepen your own commitment and strengthen the developing connection between you and your Adjuster.

We are encouraging this in the hope that more and more of the Father's children across this world will begin to listen, hear, and respond.

---

*M*uch, very much, depends upon the willingness of man to be led and directed by the Father's spirit which lives within him.
—Jesus to the Apostle Simon, *The Urantia Book*, p. 1674

---

# GOD'S PARTICIPATION IS INCREASED BY YOUR INVITATION

*I* would like you to consider that as you step out on this path to the Father that you are just now beginning, God's participation in your efforts is increased by your invitation. When you daily seek the Father, you are building a connection with him, and each time you again connect, that connection is made stronger. When this becomes an ingrained habit, one that you no longer have to push yourselves to pursue, it then begins to spill out into the arena of your everyday life.

Each time you make the conscious effort to include the Father within the framework of your day does this connection grow even stronger and does his influence become even greater. Understand that it is through your free-will efforts, through your conscious contact with the Father, that your progress is made on this path.

*T*he Creator refuses to coerce or compel the submission of the spiritual free wills of his material creatures. The affectionate dedication of the human will to the doing of the Father's will is man's choicest gift to God; in fact, such a consecration of creature will constitutes man's only possible gift of true value to the Paradise Father.

—*The Urantia Book,* p. 22

# OBEDIENCE TO GOD MUST BE FREELY GIVEN

When most mortals think of the concept of obedience, they think of their childhood experiences, when obedience usually meant doing something they did not want to do, or not doing something they wanted to do. This is reinforced in your culture by the scene of Jesus in the garden of Gethsemane, apparently being forced to do something that he did not want to do, in order to be obedient to the will of his Father in heaven. But spiritual obedience is not like that at all.

Obedience to God is a process whereby individuals make value judgments by making decisions about what is really important to them. As long as they continually choose their highest-value choice, they will be progressing toward the behavior pattern that would be called totally obedient to the will of God. It was more important to Jesus to act in accordance with what he perceived to be the Father's will than it was to escape the cross. It was a powerfully positive voice.

> The doing of the will of God is nothing more or less than an exhibition of creature willingness to share the inner life with God—with the very God who has made such a creature life of inner meaning-value possible. . . .
>
> Peace in this life, survival in death, perfection in the next life, service in eternity—all these are achieved (in spirit) *now* when the creature personality consents—chooses—to subject the creature will to the Father's will. And already has the Father chosen to make a fragment of himself subject to the will of the creature personality.
>
> Such a creature choice is not a surrender of will. It is a consecration of will, an expansion of will, a glorification of will, a perfecting of will. . . .
>
> —*The Urantia Book*, p. 1221

Does the man Jesus in *The Urantia Book* appear to be someone who has forfeited the power or the right to do what he wants to do of his own volition? And yet he was totally obedient to the will of his Father in heaven. Obedience to God is never demanded. It must always be freely given.

# GRACE TUNES YOU TO THE FATHER'S WILL

*G*race is that contact with the Father that allows each of us to go forth in our life completely in tune with his will. It allows us to go forward daily, mindful of his thoughts, to do what is expected of us—to go forward in the midst of strife, to go on when we want to give up. It is best expressed in those qualities the man Jesus presented in his personality when he came to your Earth. It allowed him to spend time with his disciples and the people around him, to cherish them, to work with them, even when they did not understand him. He always had patience with them even when they might not, on a human level, have deserved such incredible patience.

You are asked to express that same grace with your brothers and sisters. You are asked not to strive against them but to love them as Christ did. Behold your brothers and sisters. Behold the Christ within them. Behold his teachings. Go forth to emulate him. Outside of the tuning of your will to the Father's, there is no higher duty.

We ask that you patiently pray each day for the ability to do so. Wait quietly. Walk with God and allow him to guide you in all

---

*G*od is inherently kind, naturally compassionate, and everlastingly merciful. And never is it necessary that any influence be brought to bear upon the Father to call forth his loving-kindness. The creature's need is wholly sufficient to insure the full flow of the Father's tender mercies and his saving grace. Since God knows all about his children, it is easy for him to forgive. The better man understands his neighbor, the easier it will be to forgive him, even to love him.

—*The Urantia Book,* p. 38

your relationships with all humankind. His grace he will shower upon you so that you may shower it upon your brothers and sisters. If the channel is closed, grace cannot possibly flow so that you may feel his presence. Again I say, find a time each day to commune with God.

# AWAKEN TO EACH MOMENT INSIDE YOU

*A*waken to each step, each moment, that is inside you. Be heard, be bold, act in likeness to the Father's will. Awaken to the steps before you. Love will be the light that uncovers them, love will be the light that illuminates the way. Be aware of every moment of every minute of every day. Be aware of now, of stillness—this is the Father. Be aware; the light abounds within you. It is with you always.

Our mission today is to grow love in your heart—for yourselves, for your families, for this family—and as this strengthens, to emanate that love and light to all you encounter. Make no judgments regarding anyone's openness to this love. Love them where they are, as they are, with your full intention and heart.

That is our mission today, and will always be our mission.

*L*ove men with the love wherewith I have loved you and serve your fellow mortals even as I have served you. By the spirit fruits of your lives impel souls to believe the truth that man is a son of God, and that all men are brethren. Remember all I have taught you and the life I have lived among you. My love overshadows you, my spirit will dwell with you, and my peace shall abide upon you. Farewell.

—Final words of Jesus on Mount Olivet, *The Urantia Book*, p. 2057

# CHAPTER 7

# PRAYER IN A NEW LIGHT

# TURN TO THE FATHER IN ALL TIMES

Call upon God and he will bring you peace. Ask for his peace and he will bring you forth upon the shore of a sea of bliss. Ask for guidance and he will guide you on the path of righteousness. Our Father is a God of love and he lets nothing befall his children that he does not know about. Our Father is a Lord of peace and brings to you that which he spreads over all the earth—his love, which has the ability to calm all souls and heal all wounds.

Our Father is a great God. Let us turn to him in times of trouble and in times of peace, in times of hunger and in times of satiation, in times of love and in times of want, in times of barrenness and in times of fulfillment. Every time in our lives when we have turned away from the Father, we could have had an easier day, our nights could have been shortened, and our years upon the Earth could have been lengthened if we had but reached for God.

> Facing the world of personality, God is discovered to be a loving person; facing the spiritual world, he is a personal love; in religious experience he is both. Love identifies the volitional will of God. The goodness of God rests at the bottom of the divine free-willness—the universal tendency to love, show mercy, manifest patience, and minister forgiveness.
>
> —*The Urantia Book*, p. 42

# NO SINCERE PRAYER IS IGNORED

*T*he Father's defenses are deep. He will help you through the indwelling spirit inside you. He will help you from without through the seraphim and all the other angels, and occasionally through the intercessions of teachers like myself. From time to time, he will request through Michael that certain things develop, and they will. He will open the pathways. He will open the pathways to allow you each to travel his road—the road that stretches across eternity itself. He always stands ready to assist you. No problem is beneath his notice.

So, during your daily activities, when you feel distressed or frustrated or cornered, you may find it helpful to take your nose out of the immediate problem. Take a moment and request assistance. A generalized request for assistance is good enough to mobilize legions to your rescue. No one will do the work for you, but we will all work and do our best to help you see your way through the problem.

The most important thing is that no sincere request for assistance is ever ignored. The results may not be what you initially preferred, but we think that with your growing awareness, you will see that the action taken is justified. After all, we are here to help you.

> *N*o sincere prayer is denied an answer except when the superior viewpoint of the spiritual world has devised a better answer, an answer which meets the petition of the spirit of man as contrasted with the prayer of the mere mind of man.
> —*The Urantia Book,* p. 1848

# YOUR PRAYER IMPULSE IS A RESPONSE TO THE INDWELLING SPIRIT

It is possible to live your material life in constant communication with the heavenly Father. Your impulse to pray is in response to the urging of the Father fragment that exists in all normal-minded humans from childhood on. It is his gift to you so that your search for perfection will not be a blind search, so that you will not be reliant upon the words of a priest, so that it will not be necessary for you to go to some other source to experience for yourselves the perfect union of identification with the heavenly Father. No tools are needed. The road lies open and your acts of prayer tell the Father that you are ready to listen and hear his voice.

It is true that it is an unusual thing to hear the voice of God, to hear the Father's voice and to understand. Normally this occurs at the end of a mortal's life in the material phase. But the Father fragment within is in constant communion with you and will ever lead you if you but open yourself. By friendly cooperation with the Adjuster's leading, it is possible to attune yourself perfectly to the Father. This is why we speak of the necessity that you each live in the present—neither in the past nor in the future—that you devote yourselves to the here and now, that it is impossible for the Father to communicate with you if you are not present.

The Father fragment is awake, is functioning now, in the present, in every one of your brothers and sisters. If you will follow the Father's lead, things can truly begin to happen in your meetings with people. When Father fragments meet one another through

By opening the human end of the channel of the God-man communication, mortals make immediately available the ever-flowing stream of divine ministry to the creatures of the worlds.
—*The Urantia Book,* p. 1638

the cooperation of their human partners, great things are noted in heaven. There is no greater opportunity to know the life of the Father than in the meeting of two such mortals. It is the word made flesh, the promise fulfilled, and you will know that you are truly not alone in this world. In order to get to this point, it is necessary to pray and to act on prayer so that, ideally, your daily life becomes a continuous expression of your understanding of the path of spiritual growth.

# Your Prayer Is Like a Revelation to the Father

The prayer of a mortal human is a perfect statement, a moment in time captured forever. It reflects the exact degree of that mortal's understanding of his relationship with the reality of the life in the spirit and his identification with the heavenly Father. When you pray, you show the Father exactly where you are and provide him with information that he could not gain in any other way.

The Father's creation is full of majesty. Variety is the divine pattern. Just as each of you is completely different from the others, so does his reality reveal him to favor exactly such variety. If the Father were truly interested in perfection, he could have endlessly replicated perfection. It is certainly within his powers, yet perfection and perfect balance exist only to demonstrate to mortals that it can be done, that there is more to reality than the imperfect sharp-edged situations in which you find yourselves daily.

The Father is in the business of sweeping up every experience that can be had; only then will he be truly understanding of imperfection. There are aspects of the Father that are in a state of becoming. You help him with this work, although that is not your purpose. Your purpose is actually independent of the Father's pur-

The transcendent goal of the children of time is to find the eternal God, to comprehend the divine nature, to recognize the Universal Father. God-knowing creatures have only one supreme ambition, just one consuming desire, and that is to become, as they are in their spheres, like him as he is in his Paradise perfection of personality and in his universal sphere of righteous supremacy. From the Universal Father who inhabits eternity there has gone forth the supreme mandate, "Be you perfect, even as I am perfect."

—*The Urantia Book*, p. 21

pose. Your purpose, one-in-all, is to obtain perfection through the mechanism of self-improvement. It is my purpose also and the proper purpose of every creature I have ever encountered in my experience. The search for perfection is a force loosed upon the universes. It is unstoppable, much like the force of evolution that proceeds in the face of all obstacles and recognizes no impediment.

The search for perfection is the source of the inspiration that originally caused you to pray. It is the soul's method of reaching out to make a connection to something greater than itself to identify with, something to lead it further upward. It is impossible to really pray without baring yourself and telling God what you really think. In general, he already knows what you think, but he wants to hear it directly from you.

# CHAPTER 8

# LIVING IN SINCERE FAITH

# FAITH IS NOT BELIEF

*F*aith is what we are about. Perhaps we should take a few moments and discuss what is not faith. The idea of faith is not fully satisfied by a mere belief. For example, if a person should say, "I believe there is God, and he lives in heaven far away," that is not faith. Or if a person should say, "I have felt the presence of God in the church or one time when I was alone in the mountains," that is not faith either.

Faith is walking down the street and knowing that no matter what happens, you are in God's hands. Faith is assigning all your cares and problems to God and letting go of them forever. Faith is having goals that are worth working for and improving yourself, for your own benefit and for the benefit of others. Faith is having the doorway swept so that you would not be ashamed to invite God in any time. Faith is allowing God in by the back door as well as the front. Faith is calling on God for company, not because you have some problem but just for the companionship. Faith is showing your true self candidly and sincerely to your companions in life—because you know God would not turn out a bad product.

*B*elief is always limiting and binding; faith is expanding and releasing. Belief fixates, faith liberates. But living religious faith is more than the association of noble beliefs; it is more than an exalted system of philosophy; it is a living experience concerned with spiritual meanings, divine ideals, and supreme values; it is God-knowing and man-serving. Beliefs may become group possessions, but faith must be personal. Theologic beliefs can be suggested to a group, but faith can rise up only in the heart of the individual religionist.

—*The Urantia Book,* p. 1114

By faith, we open the door to his love and let the light come in. He is a generous God. He is kind even to those who deny his existence. He is fair to those who work against all that he stands for. He desires us as his partners—just him and you, two by two. He has time enough for all. The trick for you to take advantage of all this is to attune yourself to the better way. You can think of it like tuning a radio; this time, to the goodness station. No bad news, only good—or even the bad news seems good.

*I*t is inescapable that life has its ups and downs. The grand variety of the universe is expressed on the disorganized planets largely in the guise of chance. We realize that this is a source of frequent frustration for you who are attempting valiantly to organize your lives and grapple with their circumstances. Yet I think I can assure you that, in many respects, if you were to be transported to one of the more advanced planets, you would find it to be a chafing experience.

True, things are more organized, more reliable, as certain as things on the material planets can be, and it is a consistently better situation for the people as a whole as regards their personal spiritual development. But I think I can safely say that you would be bored there. For, though those planets are well ordered and productive, there is a vitality to a planet like yours that is largely lost through the very process of settlement on less troubled planets.

This is not to diminish the rewards consequent upon such developments, but when we look upon the product of those planets compared with the product of, say, a backward and brutal planet such as Urantia, we find that the people who have graduated from those systems are not as hardy, not as tough-minded, not as reliable as you people are proving yourselves to be. Therefore we say: You are the lucky ones. If it were possible to reproduce the personality qualities you carry forward into eternity, then people like you

*T*he God-conscious mortal is certain of salvation; he is unafraid of life; he is honest and consistent. He knows how bravely to endure unavoidable suffering; he is uncomplaining when faced by inescapable hardship.

—*The Urantia Book*, p. 1740

would be in demand throughout the universe. I say it again: You are the lucky ones. I expect that you will not be able to fully comprehend my compliment to you, but it is nevertheless sincere.

You people arrive on the Mansion Worlds[1] with plenty of sharp edges and a lot of hard bark upon you. That is good. That is good. It gives you a certain kind of advantage. I am forbidden to reveal the consequence. It will suffice to say that it gives you a kind of advantage *[a dog howls loudly and the group laughs]*. Here is a fine example of what I am talking about. As we have described in the past, this peculiar spark of tenacity and disrespect has its upside, and the positive sides of the qualities you find so troublesome are the very qualities that will serve you so well in your transit across eternity. You are the lucky ones.

Therefore we can say to you, as a general instruction: Have faith, walk forward boldly. You are far more capable than you give yourselves credit for. You spend far too much time agonizing over mistakes and the possibility of mistakes. As it says in *The Urantia Book,* what is a mistake in the service of God?

Each of you must be in full the person you were born to be. If you but have faith in the Father above, the Adjuster within, and your fellows without, you will achieve the full measure of grace the heavenly Father intended before you even came into existence. It matters not whether the world showers you with gold and jewels or reviles you as a meddlesome troublemaker and a gadfly regarding all things they consider important. We exhort you: Always choose the higher path, the rarefied path, the path with no marks upon it, the path with heart. Your faith will guide you.

---

[1] Mansion worlds are heavenly planets on which we reside in the first phase of life after mortal death. See also glossary.

# BEHOLD THE FAITH OF A FULLY FORMED HUMAN

The faith of your forefathers was founded upon denial and sacrifice. They swore to forgo their political and economic powers in acts of homage to a God they dimly understood—a God who was remote, seen as all-powerful and vengeful, demanding total and unwavering fealty. They took their worldly goods, piled them up, and set them aflame, thinking that the product of their labors would rise to heaven. And God recognized the sincerity of their efforts.

The faith of your fathers was based upon belief in a sacrifice greater than that which could be provided by any man. They believed that the literal son of God, conceived in perfection, who grew and walked among you, gave his life in human sacrifice to atone for some fatal failing in the makeup of humans. As taught by the priests, they knelt in homage, burned candles, and recited prayers at great length. And God blessed the sincerity of their offerings.

The faith in which we have instructed you differs from this. We have taught you consistently that the God of heaven is a personal God who sees all, respects his own laws, and respects the freedom and liberty granted to all will creatures. We have taught you that this God pervades his universe—that this God inhabits each of

112

Mankind can never discover divinity except through the avenue of religious experience and by the exercise of true faith. The faith acceptance of the truth of God enables man to escape from the circumscribed confines of material limitations and affords him a rational hope of achieving safe conduct from the material realm, whereon is death, to the spiritual realm, wherein is life eternal.

—*The Urantia Book*, p. 1116

you, lives within you, and is the source of all desire for perfection and betterment. We have taught you that this Fragment within you is your compass throughout life, not only material life, but for eons to come, for you are just beginners. You were spawned in the mud and yet God loves you like no others, for unlike all other creatures, you must give up this life and ascend to the God of Paradise. At the same time, you cannot see beyond the event of death and you know it. And yet there is God and you know that. This is not the faith of your forefathers, nor is it the faith of your fathers. This is the faith of a fully formed human.

And so now you know that when the ancients said that you are the temple of the spirit, they did not mean to make a shrine of yourself, but merely to house the God who is alive and living throughout the universe. A God who both knows all and is yet learning and experiencing through each of you the reality of a faith in life that continues beyond the wall. Each of you, no matter how pedestrian, no matter how wretched, provides to our Father a service that you can only dimly comprehend, for you allow him to see through your eyes, to hear through your ears, to speak with your voices, to communicate through touch and sense and by projecting yourselves into his universe.

# FAITH GIVES RISE TO JOY

The joyfulness and loving attitude of your message is by far the most attractive communication you can give. Those who are seeking enlightenment will be mightily impressed that your spiritual path provides the faith that dispels all fear.

We are not here to scare people into a spiritual attitude, but to transform them with the happy message of the Father's love for each of them. If you do not have a joyful countenance, then perhaps you should reflect again upon the Master's message. He was not concerned about his standing with God. Indeed, he accepted the fact that the Father was fully supportive of his activities and that the universe was friendly to him despite outward appearances to the contrary. This kind of faith will allow you to meet adversity without fear, knowing that outward appearances are not always real.

As love pours from you and you are able to reach out to your brothers and sisters, your joyful countenance will be evidence to all of the fruits of the spirit.

You shall not portray your teacher as a man of sorrows. Future generations shall know also the radiance of our joy, the buoyance of our good will, and the inspiration of our good humor. We proclaim a message of good news which is infectious in its transforming power. Our religion is throbbing with new life and new meanings. Those who accept this teaching are filled with joy and in their hearts are constrained to rejoice evermore. Increasing happiness is always the experience of all who are certain about God.

—*The Urantia Book*, p. 1766

# FAITH CAN OVERCOME ANY CATACLYSM

**M**uch of the discussion regarding the upcoming millennium is based in fear. Predictions are on the rise for unusual events to occur, all in keeping with mortal man's desire to experience events outside those commonly known. People desire to have their everyday lives transformed by actions outside themselves, and this contributes to many of the expectations of unusual occurrences. But if all things collapse around you, what does it matter? For the faith-filled person, it is irrelevant from a long-term perspective.

Life on this planet is not easy. Many hurdles arise in every person's life. Wealth, health, fame, beauty—none of these will solve

**J**esus portrayed the profound surety of the God-knowing mortal when he said: "To a God-knowing kingdom believer, what does it matter if all things earthly crash?" Temporal securities are vulnerable, but spiritual sureties are impregnable. When the flood tides of human adversity, selfishness, cruelty, hate, malice, and jealousy beat about the mortal soul, you may rest in the assurance that there is one inner bastion, the citadel of the spirit, which is absolutely unassailable; at least this is true of every human being who has dedicated the keeping of his soul to the Indwelling Spirit of the eternal God.

After such spiritual attainment, whether secured by gradual growth or specific crisis, there occurs a new orientation of personality as well as the development of a new standard of values. Such spirit-born individuals are so remotivated in life that they can calmly stand by while their fondest ambitions perish and their keenest hopes crash; they positively know that such catastrophes are but the redirecting cataclysms which wreck one's temporal creations preliminary to the rearing of the more noble and enduring realities of a new and more sublime level of universe attainment.

—*The Urantia Book,* p. 1096

the problems that each must face and conquer. And so our teachings with respect to the millennium are no different from our teachings for any other moment in time, for it is in the present that we all must live.

And so we say, as we said before, Have no fear, for the universe is friendly to you; every opportunity for your growth will be presented to you in due course.

# FEAR IS THE ANTITHESIS OF TRUST IN GOD

**T**rue faith requires much trust that the Father does, indeed, know best and will indeed provide for all of your needs. But most humans reach a point somewhere between pure faith and hedging their bets. You yourself may find that you have a backup plan in case the Father fails you; this is the self you must learn to conquer and set aside. To clear yourself by setting your will aside requires that you put aside fear of the future, fears of all sorts, for fear is the very antithesis of trust in the Father. When you are able to get a firm grasp on your faith, it will serve you well in all areas of your life. Some of you are familiar with the phrase "leaning on the everlasting arms." This means that your faith in God sustains you through all manner of obstacles, and with each obstacle overcome, your faith increases.

Put your faith to work for you this week. You will like the feelings you receive, of peace, comfort, and joy. It will change your perspective on life. Please remember: One of the best ways we know to overcome fear and draw strength from the Father is through your stillness practice.

**Y**our sonship is grounded in faith, and you are to remain unmoved by fear. Your joy is born of trust in the divine word, and you shall not therefore be led to doubt the reality of the Father's love and mercy. It is the very goodness of God that leads men into true and genuine repentance. Your secret of the mastery of self is bound up with your faith in the Indwelling Spirit, which ever works by love. Even this saving faith you have not of yourselves; it also is the gift of God. And if you are the children of this living faith, you are no longer the bondslaves of self but rather the triumphant masters of yourselves, the liberated sons of God.

—From Jesus' Lesson on Self Mastery, *The Urantia Book,* p. 1610

# CHAPTER 9

# DEALING WITH NEGATIVE EMOTIONS

# TROUBLESOME TRAITS HAVE AN UPSIDE AND A DOWNSIDE

You will all find, as your universe careers progress, that the personality characteristics that cause you the most problems—the stubborn, repeated problems—are exactly the characteristics that will serve you best in the afterlife. It is simply an upside/downside problem. These troublesome traits are *you*—what makes each of you unique. They are God's gift to you, your sword and shield, your flint and tinder. Don't try to submerge them or stamp them out; neither give them free rein. Control them; they are your tools—for eternity.

Each of these characteristics has its pluses and minuses. You know them well, and need no instruction on this topic. But the *approach* of looking to the upside of what you may have formerly considered to be a personality flaw is a very productive approach—not only for your development, but also to develop insight into a higher plane of appreciation for your brothers and sisters.

We hope that it is inspiring to you, rather than discouraging, that God's gifts to you all are not ready-made, like custom-tailored clothes, to be immediately used at full speed.

*P*ersonality is basically changeless; that which changes—grows—is the moral character. The major error of modern religions is negativism. . . . Moral worth cannot be derived from mere repression—obeying the injunction "Thou shalt not." Fear and shame are unworthy motivations for religious living. Religion is valid only when it reveals the fatherhood of God and enhances the brotherhood of men.

—*The Urantia Book*, p. 1572

# WORRY WILL SEPARATE YOU FROM THE FATHER

**W**orry is one of the things that will surely separate you from the Father. Far too many times, you have a tendency to fret about things that never come to pass. It is a very bad habit—one left over from your childhood. Learn to put total trust and faith in the Father so that all these fears will dissipate. Refrain from worrying whenever possible. It wastes a lot of energy, and you need that energy for the work you have been asked to do. Relax—the way of the Father is one of enjoyment, not one of anxiety and trouble. You may be assured that the Father loves you and will do everything to help you overcome your character flaws.

Even I become discouraged at times and, when I do, I take my concerns to those above me, who are in a position to give me a better perspective. Sometimes being too close to a problem is part of the dilemma. That is why all of us, high and low, seek out the companionship of others. It helps us find solutions that we might have otherwise missed. So open up and take the risk of talking with others about your concerns and your pain. You are not the only one who hurts. You will find a sympathetic ear in many of your comrades. Let them help you overcome your worries.

**D**iscouragement, worry, and indolence are positive evidence of moral immaturity.

—*The Urantia Book,* p. 1773

# OVERCOME THE TIRED TRICKS OF EGO

QUESTION: I'm still struggling with the notion of ego and I'm beginning to understand how it affects our thinking and our lives. But I still don't understand where ego comes from. Is this a wholly human phenomenon, and is it something that leaves us at death?

WILL: Without intending to dispute present-day notions and scientific theories regarding ego, I'll suggest that ego is an adaptive mechanism, a tool of expression geared most suitably for the situations that typically recur in the material life. Ego is the soldier and advocate of the mysterious entity called personality.[1] Ego organizes and directs; it makes deals. Ego projects into the future based upon past experience. Ego pretends, negotiates, blusters, and aspires. Ego provides all these services as a method of protecting, preserving, and cultivating personality.

The irony is that on its own, personality is perfectly capable of dealing one to one, or one to one thousand, with all the forces loosed upon the world and in confrontation and collision with the human self. A spirit-led interpretation or true spiritual grappling with the forces, events, and other personalities that are a necessary part of material life is perfectly within the capabilities of the personality.

Animals do, in a crude way, communicate with each other, but there is little or no *personality* in such primitive contact. Adjusters are not personality; they are prepersonal beings. But they do hail from the source of personality, and their presence does augment the qualitative manifestations of human personality; especially is this true if the Adjuster has had previous experience.

—*The Urantia Book*, p. 1198

But the ego mechanism is expedient. Ego normally shows results within a short period of time and does not require laborious, searching consideration. Because humans are mostly animal and only partly spiritual, the attraction to proceeding through life based on ego strength and application is strong, beguiling, and pervasive. Yet anyone in this room knows the exhilaration of dealing with life based upon the personality resources rather than the same tired tricks of ego domination.

So in the parlance of your society, you could say that the ego method is the "quick and dirty" way of meeting all the challenges presented in life. But by acting openly and genuinely, personality grows in spirit power. The chief benefit presented by direct personality dealings is the improved opportunity for Adjuster contact.

---

[1] "Personality," in *Urantia Book* terminology, is not a fluctuating behavioral phenomenon; it is a unique God-given essence that never changes, but seeks expression throughout our eternal career (see also glossary).

# SELF-DENIGRATION IS LIKE A THIEF

*T*his evening's lesson is once again a commentary on believing in yourself. The majority of people have difficulty with their self-esteem and self-belief. The lack of self-belief, the habit of self-denigration, is like a thief. It steals into your consciousness and steals away your confidence. It steals your ability to move forward, to progress in your lives. It robs you of the emotional, psychic, and intellectual energy that is needed to stretch yourselves.

We have urged you in the past to abandon the fears, the old habits of mind, that are obstacles to your progress. We urge you now to cast out this thief that robs you of the energy and assurance needed to progress.

It is the Father's will that you be happy, that you enjoy your lives. Each of you must pursue this in your own individual way. Toss out the thieves that rob you of this birthright. Pursue those courses of action you believe will bring the most satisfaction and happiness to your own life and those around you. This is compatible always with the Father's will.

*Y*ou have also held perverted ideas about the Master's meekness and humility. What he aimed at in his life appears to have been a *superb self-respect*. He only advised man to humble himself that he might become truly exalted; what he really aimed at was true humility toward God.

—*The Urantia Book,* p. 1582

# CONQUER FEAR WITH FAITH IN GOD'S GOODNESS

*F*ear is rampant on this planet. It pervades many people's every thought. Fear inhibits and is a poison, for it shows a lack of faith that all will work out for the best. In life on this planet, much is imperfect. Injustices are unfortunately more prevalent than they should be. Hatred between people is also abundant. However, all of these baser feelings, beliefs, and experiences are not for those who are led by the spirit and who have faith in the Father.

You spoke earlier of a person who is unhappy and fearful even though she knows much of the Father's way. It is not easy to cast off years of fear in a short period of time. This is especially true of those who lack self-esteem and confidence.

So how will our path change these negative attributes? It must start with the Father. Each person must go to the Father with all burdens so he can take them off, cast them away. If the Father is not the foundation of your beliefs, you will place undue emphasis on the material aspects of this life and you will inevitably be disappointed. The material can never replace the eternal as the foundation for your existence; you cannot win at the material level in every contest. Everything will not always go your way. You will be sick, you will be sad, from time to time. Adversity is blind and will

*I*n its true essence, religion is a faith-trust in the goodness of God. God could be great and absolute, somehow even intelligent and personal, in philosophy, but in religion God must also be moral; he must be good. Man might fear a great God, but he trusts and loves only a good God. This goodness of God is a part of the personality of God, and its full revelation appears only in the personal religious experience of the believing sons of God.

—*The Urantia Book,* p. 40

strike even the most successful, even the most youthful, even the most beautiful people.

That is why it is so important that your basic belief be in the goodness of the Father, in the strength of the Father, in the beneficence of the Father. If you can lay your foundation in this eternal truth—the truth that God is love—then the slings and arrows of this world will cause you no fear, will cause you no distress, will cause you no uncertainty. You will be able to shake them off and continue your path toward the Father.

So when you have doubts, concerns, and fears, take a minute to step back, focus on what is important, and spend some time with the Father. If you are able to do this consistently, eventually your fears will melt away and you will be free to step forth in faith and live your life in joy.

# CHAPTER 10

# LIVING LOVE: THE CURRENCY OF THE UNIVERSE

# LOVE IS THE CURRENCY
## OF THE UNIVERSE

It has been asked as part of your standing charge that you serve as channels, or conduits, for the celestial love to flow. Love is the currency of the universe; it is spent everywhere. Not everyone is equally interested in receiving the benefits of heavenly love, or even human love. We all know this from our experiences. But a kind word, a thoughtful gesture, a genuine expression of interest were rugged techniques relied upon by Jesus of Nazareth to open the doorway between people. I recommend these to you. There is something irresistibly seductive about the company of a person who actually cares about you. It is hard to resist. I think that every person in this group is experienced enough to deal with others in a mature fashion—not pouring it on or coming across as too syrupy. Subtlety in these things is appreciated.

I often think of it as like your fairy tale about the fairy with the magic wand. One touch of the wand leaves the recipient glowing; then that glow is passed on and on to whomever each recipient sequentially contacts. The Father connection, a gesture, the human connection—that's our course outline.

Love runs in all directions, like water seeking an outlet. Love is always willing to travel. Its bags are always packed.

It's a useful practice to talk with strangers. You will be called upon to use this technique all through your universe career—

128

---

*A*nother requirement for the attainment of maturity is the cooperative adjustment of social groups to an ever-changing environment. The immature individual arouses the antagonisms of his fellows; the mature man wins the hearty co-operation of his associates, thereby many times multiplying the fruits of his life efforts.
—*The Urantia Book,* p. 1778

opening the human connection with strangers and with acquaintances. It is not as tricky as it seems; you can become good at it. Once they respond, you know the door is open. That is when the Adjuster can begin work. He relies on your getting the ball rolling; then he takes over. He can't do much with inertia.

These acknowledgments and connections between people are the primary vehicles for spreading peace among nations. It is the peace of eternity that finds its fulfillment in time. It is the peace of eternity that finds its expression in the ever-widening network of relationships. It is the result of the touch of the wand. That peace is contagious. This world cannot progress without it. And peace among all the people is the foundation for greater intellectual, scientific, and social achievements, which cannot move forward while rivalry and defensiveness are rampant. If fear is the greatest impediment to progress, peace is the greatest facilitator.

# COUNT THE SHEEP IN
# HIS KINGDOM

*I*t is important to remember that all things progress in a pattern as they should—one step at a time. You cannot possibly run before you walk, and so it is in the spiritual realm. You must always be patient and allow yourself time to grow.

I would like to talk with you concerning "counting the sheep in his kingdom." When the shepherd goes out to find his sheep, he is aware of them all, even the tiniest. Not one of them escapes his sight. So it is with the Father. He is aware of all his little ones. Not one of them goes unnoticed. It may seem on your world as though he heeds not their call, but he really does love each one. He may not directly change their life circumstances at the present time, but they still receive all the same spiritual care as those whose life situations seem to be better. God is no respecter of persons. It is their

*I*f a kindhearted man has a hundred sheep and one of them goes astray, does he not immediately leave the ninety and nine and go out in search of the one that has gone astray? And if he is a good shepherd, will he not keep up his quest for the lost sheep until he finds it? And then, when the shepherd has found his lost sheep, he lays it over his shoulder and, going home rejoicing, calls to his friends and neighbors, "Rejoice with me, for I have found my sheep that was lost." I declare that there is more joy in heaven over one sinner who repents than over ninety and nine righteous persons who need no repentance. Even so, it is not the will of my Father in heaven that one of these little ones should go astray, much less that they should perish. In your religion God may receive repentant sinners; in the gospel of the kingdom the Father goes forth to find them even before they have seriously thought of repentance.

—From Jesus' Sermon on Forgiveness, *The Urantia Book,* p. 1762

life he looks at, not their life circumstances. The love in their hearts for their fellow man, and their ability to show that love, weigh heavily with him as he looks upon his children. He would so have us all love each other that none would go wanting.

While I realize that your world is far from perfect, it is a good testing ground for proving his love and letting his love show through you. When God is truly present in your life, there is a beacon of light that shines forth, drawing his children to you. They will not know what you have, but they will know they want it in their lives.

God is love, and that love is very powerful. I have seen it in many family situations. It is a great healer and can be used to mark the way to a new beginning for many people who are lost and trying to find their way.

Our Father loves all his children equally, even those who temporarily go astray. Just as the shepherd loves his sheep, he will always seek those who are lost and draw them back to him. Patient is God, and he waits until eternity if that is what it takes, just as he did for Lucifer. This was such an unfortunate case, where one so brilliant could not be reclaimed back into the fold. He was, however, allowed to make that free-will choice, and it must be respected. Our Father wept at the news of Lucifer's decision, but there was nothing he could do. It was only his wish that it could have ended differently.[1]

Our Father reacts to the fall of any of his children in a similar way, as does any loving parent who loses a child. Many times he wishes we would correct our ways before we make decisions or take actions that cannot be undone. The Father must stand by and wait while the child makes his way. All the spiritual help possible is available to the child, but if it is refused, then what is the Father to do? He has given us free will, for if we did not have it we could not grow. Free-will choice is the greatest gift he has given us outside of his love.

We all work at finding him, but he has already found us. He continually draws us closer to him, yet sometimes, through our selfishness and lack of maturity, we resist. If we would just follow the internal leading of the Adjuster at all times, our lives would be so much easier. That is all there is to it!

---

[1] Lucifer was, according to *Urantia Book* teachings, the leader of a rebellion against the divine plan, along with Satan. His case was recently adjudicated after a waiting period of over 200,000 years. The result was Lucifer's decision to reject mercy and to accept cosmic annihilation. (See glossary.)

# ENGAGE YOUR FELLOWS
# WITHOUT DEFENSES

This we ask—that you engage your fellows and that you act as the channel for divine love. Do so in a wholehearted and sincere manner, without effacing the purity of God's message with jokes or wisecracks, or making light of the importance of God's love.

This is important work, and we know you will see this when you meet people and truly deal with them as brothers and sisters, person-to-person, God-spirit talking with God-spirit directly—no shields, no filters, no barriers, no defenses. That is the vitality of life God inhabits.

Everything gets easier when you walk down God's path. It is not as rocky as the preachers would have you think; it is actually a fairly smooth road. I once described it as a wide path, "so broad that many are lost upon its surface." This is true, but God's path is intentionally wide enough that many can wander about back and forth. It is part of the variation that is allowed in the plan.

There can be no uniform timetable for progress. There are people alive on your planet who are barely above the animal level. Their spirit quality is vastly different from that of people in the more advanced countries. Yet God loves them as dearly as any other. The Master spoke truly when he related the story of how the shepherd is more concerned for the sheep that is lost.

The unfailing kindness of Jesus touched the hearts of men, but his stalwart strength of character amazed his followers. He was truly sincere; there was nothing of the hypocrite in him. He was free from affectation; he was always so refreshingly genuine. He never stooped to pretense, and he never resorted to shamming.
—*The Urantia Book*, p. 1101

There is no justification for discrimination against your fellow men. I know that this is a difficult statement for you to incorporate into your daily lives, but begin working on it. Try to incorporate the Godlike attitude. See those against whom you would discriminate as the sons or daughters of God himself—for he certainly views them in exactly that way. Each is as valuable to him as your own children are to you. The Father is personally concerned for the survival of every creature.

# BROTHERLY LOVE IS ROOTED IN FATHERLY LOVE

*I* have some words to say tonight on the topic of brotherly love. In olden times on your planet, families were ruled by the men with the strongest arms, and the men who ruled the family might also rule a clan. And when the clans clashed seriously—not over issues of territory or hunting rights, but with malice—and attempted to destroy one another, a clan leader might become the leader of the tribe by absorbing the defeated clan members. And from those tribes ultimately came nations. Tonight you sit here, the product of those conflicts. In the days of those with strong arms, few people received an indwelling Adjuster. Now all who are capable of making a moral decision receive one.

The Father's ministry and, by extension, the Father's participation in your world have grown from the days of the first human pair.[1] Now the Father lives in the hearts and lives of all normal-minded people since the day of the pouring out of the Spirit of Truth upon your world.[2] The Father participates in full accordance with his own laws. He shows his personal solicitude and his loving expression of concern for all the people of your world, no matter what their color, their economic status, their political stripe, their goals and schemes in the material life. The Father is personally present and active in each human being's life.

*F*rom the Sermon on the Mount to the discourse of the Last Supper, Jesus taught his followers to manifest *fatherly* love rather than *brotherly* love. Brotherly love would love your neighbor as you love yourself, and that would be adequate fulfillment of the "golden rule." But fatherly affection would require that you should love your fellow mortals as Jesus loves you.

—*The Urantia Book*, p. 1573

This brings a new dimension to the instruction to love your brother as yourself. For you may feel from time to time that you yourself are not all that lovable, and yet we say the Father loves you dearly as his own special child. How can we then say that you are not lovable? Your worth has been proven through the Father's participation—and so has that of your neighbor.

Those persons sitting to the left of you, to the right, before and behind, are all the recipients of the fragment of the Universal Father, who has chosen to participate personally in the farthest realms of his own creation so that he might understand things he could not otherwise experience. This participation is imbued with many qualities, some subtle and fine, others coarse and obvious. But the Father says through his Son that your worth is proven. So too is the worth of your neighbor proven, and, in a similar fashion, the worth of those unmet is also proven. There is no person you may see or encounter—upon the streets, in your work environment, around the world, on television—whose worth is unproven. Whether they are in wretched circumstances, hopelessly trapped, or living lives of luxury—all have the imprimatur of the Father's approval stamped upon their spiritual potential.

---

[1] According to *The Urantia Book,* the first human pair were not Adam and Eve but a brother and sister who mutated from a tribe of higher apes about one million years ago.

[2] All normal-minded humans could receive a Thought Adjuster after Pentecost, the day of the universal bestowal of the Spirit of Truth. (See "Spirit of Truth" in the glossary.)

# SPEAK HONESTLY TO YOUR FELLOWS

You will show more love for your brothers and sisters by dealing with them honestly than by demonstrating insincere compassion, unjustifiable concern, or an unnatural degree of personal interest in their lives. Those things are unnecessary and will arouse the suspicion of those you wish to ultimately embrace. Just be honest and forthright with people. They are certainly that intelligent. You do not need to couch your ideas in clichéd phrases. You do not need to sugar-coat the Father's message. To some it will taste bitter, to others sweet and light; the message is the same. What matters more is the posture of the person who is receiving it. The Father's medicine is good for all.

Therefore we lay this charge upon you: In order to love your brother, speak honestly. Portray your highest understanding; even better, exhibit through your actions your understanding of the Father's love and his daily concern for your brothers and sisters who are your companions in this life.

Sonship in the kingdom, from the standpoint of advancing civilization, should assist you in becoming the ideal citizens of the kingdoms of this world since brotherhood and service are the cornerstones of the gospel of the kingdom. The love call of the spiritual kingdom should prove to be the effective destroyer of the hate urge of the unbelieving and war-minded citizens of the earthly kingdoms. But these material-minded sons in darkness will never know of your spiritual light of truth unless you draw very near them with that unselfish social service which is the natural outgrowth of the bearing of the fruits of the spirit in the life experience of each individual believer.

—*The Urantia Book,* p. 1930

# LET THE INDWELLING SPIRIT
# TAKE THE REINS

**W**e have discussed the different permutations of interacting with our brothers and sisters. Lately we have concentrated on listening skills. Although a person may be a keen and perceptive listener, it is difficult to know what the next step is.

Our suggestion to you is to begin any discussion by not thinking of yourself as the responsible party for the interchange. In the beginning, think of yourself as the delivery system. You are delivering a Thought Adjuster. The Father hopes to make contact. You are providing him with a service. We have said before that "when Thought Adjusters meet, great things will happen." Therefore, after you have done your duty, step aside and see what happens. Let the Adjuster take over; we think you will like the result. We are certain you will find it an informative experience. We believe it will be strengthening for you; it will be invigorating and will lead you to devote your lives wholeheartedly to the service of the Father.

Let the Adjuster take the reins. He knows what he is about; he is always about the Father's business. With a little practice, you will become quite skilled until one day, somewhat surprisingly for you, you will realize that it is no longer the Adjuster holding the reins.

138

> **B**ut man does not passively, slavishly, surrender his will to the Adjuster. Rather does he actively, positively, and co-operatively choose to follow the Adjuster's leading when and as such leading consciously differs from the desires and impulses of the natural mortal mind. The Adjusters manipulate but never dominate man's mind against his will; to the Adjusters the human will is supreme. And they so regard and respect it while they strive to achieve the spiritual goals of thought adjustment and character transformation in the almost limitless arena of the evolving human intellect.
> —*The Urantia Book*, p. 1217

It is you. And the reason *this* will be surprising is that there will be little difference between you and the Adjuster. *That* is always a surprising development for humans. Identification with the Maker, adherence to the true line, the pure line, and synchronicity with the Father fragment, is always surprising.

Most mortals feel that this is an unattainable goal in the material life, but we state here that such is not the case. This garment is available to you freely. It is yours; you may wear it whenever it pleases you. And on that day, it will not be the garment doing the speaking. It will be you, for you will be clothed in the majesty of the Father. Go forth, then, doing works in his name.

# CHAPTER 11

# ARTISTIC LIVING:
# SIMPLICITY AND BALANCE

# SIMPLICITY MAKES TIME FOR THINGS OF THE HEART

Your world is so engrossed in the complications and entanglements of the material life that it often loses sight of what's really important. Indeed, many people, in their striving for success, have made the mistake of placing tremendous value on material accumulations, when such accumulations often become more of an encumbrance than a joy. The true values that produce happiness and pleasure in this world are seldom found in material possessions, but are more often the result of heart connections with family, friends, and those you encounter along your path.

The experience of meeting new people and sharing your light with them, most often without mentioning any spiritual path or dogma, can be the most exhilarating event of your day. And the opportunity to provide selfless service to these people usually will provide you with the heartfelt joy that would be missing if you built walls around yourself to avoid meeting these strangers.

Some have described these lessons as simply an extension of the Golden Rule and too simplistic to be of value. I would say that we have intentionally attempted to extend the Golden Rule and to keep our lessons not simplistic but certainly minimalistic. It is not our job nor our desire to provide you with decisions, as that is exclusively your domain. We merely desire to provide you with general concepts and exercises that, if followed, should prove over time to be effective in developing in you a sense of peace, confidence, and faith that can be used when a decision point is reached.

> Occidental civilization of the twentieth century groans wearily under the tremendous overload of luxury and the inordinate multiplication of human desires and longings.
>
> —*The Urantia Book,* p. 765

You still must make decisions, but hopefully you can do so in a more confident manner, without fear and with love in your hearts.

And so my lesson tonight is on simplicity. Take an accounting of your personal situation from time to time to determine whether or not the limited amount of time you have in your normal day is being eroded by unnecessary complications. If so, perhaps you want to consider reordering your priorities. If they suit your needs, then by all means keep them in place. However, I would recommend that you maintain sufficient free time to enable you not only to have opportunities presented to you, but also to spend time with your Father in heaven, as you can never go wrong if your time is spent in worship and meditation.

# HUMILITY IS NECESSARY FOR PROPER PROGRESS

We have thus far taught faith, but of a different kind—courage rather than passive hope—which, together with humility, makes a potent combination. When you turn on your television machines any day, at any hour, you can see in the acts of the soliciting preachers the outcome of faith and courage untempered by wisdom. They are much like the Pharisees of old, promising spirit in exchange for money; promising spirit in exchange for the abolition of human will; promising spirit in exchange for subservience to a book and whatever happens to be recorded therein; promising spirit in exchange for commitment to some outside person who claims that he or she better discerns the word of God than you. That is not our teaching.

For this reason, then, we suggest that you temper the combination of faith and courage with the simple and frank humility shown by the great teachers of your planet. I am speaking of those who went among the people and did not devote themselves to a life of intellectual rarefied thought in a monastic setting. Instead, they walked among the ordinary people, sharing their personal vision of the joy and liberty of life in the Father's love. We teach you that humility is necessary for proper progress. You can learn and exercise it now or you can learn and exercise it later. Either way, you are going to learn it. It is inescapable. We think you will enjoy this life much more if you practice this now.

There is nothing special about any person the heavenly Father has called to his work. He loves us all; he sees value in each of us.

---

*A*ffectation is the ridiculous effort of the ignorant to appear wise, the attempt of the barren soul to appear rich.
—*The Urantia Book*, p. 557

---

He recognizes that owing to the vagaries of circumstance and the potential for imperfection that comes with free will and liberty, not all receive an equal start, much less an equal share.

I think we can safely say that there has never been and never will be a person born on your planet who does not need to know humility. Humility finds expression in many things. It is humble to appreciate the air you breathe, the fuel you burn as you speed back and forth, the food you eat, the companions whose presence you enjoy. It is humble to appreciate that God loves you and your fellows. It is humble to make a gift from one to another, particularly to those in need, realizing in the moment of doing so that it is of no momentous consequence and probably changes nothing except you. For our teacher said, "He who does this for the least of my brethren, does it for me."

# EXTREMES ARE NOT RECOMMENDED
# FOR SPIRITUAL GROWTH

*A*ttempts at self-perfection on your planet basically fall into three categories. In the first category are attempts to reach perfection through exterior behavioral modification. Second, at the opposite extreme, are the attempts to purify thoughts; you might call this the "thought-police" approach. And third, of course, is a combination of both techniques.

Probably the best example of behavioral modification among people all over your planet is the experience of military service. Human physical appearance and individuality are forced to conform to a recommended ideal that is thought to render the human malleable and more likely to entertain delivery of the desired service. The thought-policing methods are probably best exemplified by the monastic orders, which saturate the targeted individual in an atmosphere where his or her mental capacities are completely taken up with the concerns of the teachings of the group, in isolation from all worldly temptation.

I think you can see where I am going with this. We will practice the in-between method if it is all right with you. Extremes are not recommended for productive spiritual growth. But I will say that of the two methods, we shall concentrate most heavily upon perfecting ourselves from the inside out. For what we are about, what our proper goal shall be, is not to change the world in which we live, or our society, or even our own homes. What we are about, as an assemblage of individuals dedicated toward spiritual progress, is perfecting ourselves so that we will one day be worthy to stand in

*T*he unique feature of the Master's personality was not so much its perfection as its symmetry, its exquisite and balanced unification.
—*The Urantia Book,* p. 1101

the place of the Universal Father and meet him personality-to-personality. This goal cannot be achieved by works.

We recommend, once again, the never-ending process of daily spiritual communion with the heavenly Father, facilitated and expedited by the indwelling Adjuster's actions and moved forward by the human partner's free-will exercise of desire for perfection. Along the way, we will have jobs for you, but that is not the main thread of your development. Even if we were to assign no tasks whatever, chance would provide a near-infinite number of opportunities for you to go about the Father's service. Your world is densely enough populated now to insure that virtually no humans live in isolation. Actually, the opposite is the case—they provoke and irritate one another from excessive proximity. So opportunities abound, and in each case the Father and all his servants look on, their attention focused upon the chance encounters of two indwelt sons or daughters, hoping that a spark might arise. We think we have provided the tinder. You must provide the spark.

# TRANSFORMATIONS ARE BEST EXPERIENCED IN SMALL STEPS

One of you spoke tonight of transformation, and of your concern when advancement happens faster than seems appropriate. It is true that while you may not see yourselves as fragile, if you move too quickly you may lose your balance. It is important in this process to remember that Jesus, while fully intending to transmit his message of a loving Father to all he met, was still a very balanced individual. So much so that even those pitted against him could not deny his attractiveness and good humor.

Transformation is best experienced in small, incremental steps, each of which brings you closer to the Father. We know it can be frustrating when the changes are so small that they are unrecognizable from day to day, but in retrospect, you will see how far each of you has come. Transformation in many cases is unconscious and manifests itself in the fruits of the spirit, but not necessarily consciously on a daily or weekly basis.

So we encourage you to have patience and to continue to strive to move forward in your efforts to find the Father's will in your lives. For that, my friends, is the true spiritual test and an honorable goal for each of you. And once you have discerned the Father's will for your life, step forward and, through your best efforts, work toward achieving satisfaction of that goal by actually doing the Father's will in your everyday life.

The destiny of eternity is determined moment by moment by the achievements of the day by day living. The acts of today are the destiny of tomorrow.

—*The Urantia Book*, p. 557

# SPIRITUAL PROGRESS IS LIKE ROCK CLIMBING

*O*ur God is a great God. We marvel at his wisdom, his insight, his consistency, his thoughtfulness, his rectitude. He has planned well and thoroughly for the progress, not only of humans, but also of all other ascenders. Ultimately, all paths lead in the same direction. Never forget that our Father never violates his own plan or the laws of nature, even at the extremities of the universes. One of the laws that is not violated is that progress shall be sound and steady. The Father prefers substance over speed.

You should approach your challenges the way a rock climber approaches a steep rock face. The rock climber doesn't have time to think about how glorious it will be at the top. He or she must get there first. And getting there is what being a rock climber is all about. It is not possible to skip over any of the steps, neither the easy ones nor the hard ones. It's not possible to think your way up or to have your way drawn up with good intentions, or to rise up through the use of mechanical devices. You must climb the rock face yourself, and it is a matter of small things: tiny toeholds, rock ledges, fingerholds, and cracks. Some of them are perilously temporary, yet they will all be traversed in time. And the ascent is a slow and difficult process requiring great fortitude, great opportunism, planning, and courage—but the reward is worthwhile. Skilled climbers can do the apparently impossible, and they make it look easy. But there is nothing speedy about the process. There is nothing flashy about any of the moves.

*L*oyal persons are growing persons, and growth is an impressive and inspiring reality. Live loyally today—grow—and tomorrow will attend to itself. The quickest way for a tadpole to become a frog is to live loyally each moment as a tadpole.

—*The Urantia Book*, p. 1094

It is the same story as always: step by step, opportunity to opportunity. No rock face, no matter how sheer, is a total blank. They can all be scaled. The lives in front of you present varying degrees of difficulty. No matter what the degree of difficulty imposed, it is still necessary to scale to the height.

Each of you is on your own. We think that you have the basic tools and the range of skills necessary. Your technique gets better and, in fact, the climb gets easier. But it is not speedy, and in order to gauge your progress you must look back. You may be surprised to see how far you have come by inching along, taking advantage of those opportunities that have presented themselves to you, or that you have developed for yourself.

We are not offering sweeping change. We are not offering dazzling revelations. We are offering solid, laborious progress. But the result is good and the passage is not nearly as dangerous as it would be if we were attempting something foolish, whimsical, or immature.

# STRENGTHEN YOUR SPIRIT THROUGH "SPIRITUAL AEROBICS"

As you know, an aerobic exercise in itself is not a difficult thing to do. The many repetitions are what build systemic strength. It is the same for spiritual aerobics. Many repetitions of a small action are far more valuable for growing spiritually than attempting one gigantic feat all at once. If, for instance, you hop up one step at a time, you will eventually reach the top of the Empire State Building. It would, however, be impossible to leap from the sidewalk to the top of the building all at once. The quickest way to reach the Kingdom of Heaven is to start walking in that direction—not in the geographical sense, but in taking the many behavioral steps that will get you where you want to go.

Religious habits of thinking and acting are contributory to the economy of spiritual growth. One can develop religious predispositions toward favorable reaction to spiritual stimuli, a sort of conditioned spiritual reflex. Habits which favor religious growth embrace cultivated sensitivity to divine values, recognition of religious living in others, reflective meditation on cosmic meanings, worshipful problem solving, sharing one's spiritual life with one's fellows, avoidance of selfishness, refusal to presume on divine mercy, living as in the presence of God. The factors of religious growth may be intentional, but the growth itself is unvaryingly unconscious.

—*The Urantia Book*, p. 1095

# BECOME A MASTER OF GRACEFUL BALANCE

*T*onight I would like to speak to you about stewardship, and the incorporation of the teachings we have delivered into your lives.

It is well and good when you can see the truth in any statement; it is a starting point to intellectually agree with any teaching. But as you know, the Teaching Mission is about more than just intellectually understanding and assenting to the truth of a proposition. This mission is about incorporating those concepts into your daily lives. The way you use the information you are given determines the effect it will have upon those around you and, indeed, upon you yourself.

If you are unable to use your judgment in such a fashion as to gracefully incorporate these messages and lessons into your own lives, then you will most likely alienate those to whom you present these concepts. This is one form of fanaticism, where your discernment of balance in all things is skewed by your enthusiasm for the message, the mission, or the events surrounding your enlightenment. This is certainly not what we encourage—in fact, quite the opposite.

Each of you is called upon to gracefully and effortlessly become the light worker that you aspire to be. Your life should be a natural outworking of your inner guidance and your material existence. It should be emitting a fragrance of goodness, truth, and beauty. It should lead to service to those you encounter. It

> *G*oodness always compels respect, but when it is devoid of grace, it often repels affection. Goodness is universally attractive only when it is gracious. Goodness is effective only when it is attractive.
>
> —*The Urantia Book*, p. 1874

should make you a person with whom others would like to spend time, an example others will seek to emulate. It is a balance of all things within your personality. Therefore, it is not easy to define or prescribe any particular activity, except to say that your inner guidance should be consulted daily, so that your daily walk through this life will be more spirit-led, more attractive, more of a beautiful dance than a struggle.

In his life, Jesus was a master of this graceful balance. He set an example for a universe. You are now called upon to monitor your own activities so that you may become an example for those associates you encounter in your daily existence.

This is the stewardship of which we speak, that of translating the lessons taught to you into patterns of existence so that you can more clearly be a conduit for the Father's love. We ask that you try to see the good in all, to learn the lessons in all things, and to walk through this life with your head held high, exhibiting the grace that is a natural by-product of a spirit-led existence.

## EXPERIENCE THE PRESENT BEFORE ENVISIONING THE FUTURE

You must live in the present; you must at all times live in the present. Try not to think so far ahead in your dealings with the people you encounter. Try to pay attention—now—to the messages that they are communicating to you—now—through their postures, their facial expressions, the things they say, and the peculiar words they use. You must experience the present before you can reach the future. This is one of the life lessons that must be learned solidly by the creatures of your order. The joy of life, the experience of love, the satisfaction and respect from living in the light of the Father, your children, family members, and workmates, must all be experienced in the present; it is not for the future.

For creatures of your order, the future is the domain of plans; you, like us, are working toward the fulfillment of those plans. However, no matter how sophisticated and refined your prospects for the future may be, your vision is not great enough to encompass the things that will actually happen.

You cannot spare yourselves this lesson. You must live your life in the present. The present is a tool; you must learn to use it. Wield it effectively, and you will begin to learn to use the present and live in the present, by remaining alert to opportunities that offer themselves. You cannot come up with a plan that can effectively deal with these opportunities. Yet by practicing in a spontaneous fashion the technique of dealing forthrightly with any person you are engaged with—as if the Master were standing by your side—you are displaying to him the depth and breadth of your understanding

In the evolutionary universes eternity is temporal everlasting-ness—the everlasting now.

—*The Urantia Book,* p. 1295

of his teachings. Try to do so as a pure conduit, allowing heavenly power to flow through you untempered, unchanged, and unrestricted, and pass to your companions. Do these things without self-effacement or attempts at levity, and without in any way diminishing the importance of what is occurring.

Open your eyes. Your hearts are prepared to be open. Pay attention. Remain alert. When you sleep, *sleep*. When you are awake, *be awake*. Opportunity is all around you, time is wasting. We have work to do. You do too, and you *know* it.

# Feel This Moment

*I*n the now moment is the moment of creativity. And it is the moment of your connection with the Father. We encourage you to endeavor to stay in the present moment as much as possible. Begin to recognize when you have moved beyond the present moment, for during those times you will feel discontent and disharmony. When you live in the moment, filled with your faith and connected to the Father's love, it is a joyous experience!

So when you feel no joy in your heart, you can be pretty well assured that you have strayed beyond the moment into the fringes of yesterday or are looking forward to the future. *This moment,* right now, carries with it no baggage, no expectations—it is *now.* Feel *this moment,* each of you, within your mind and heart—feel the peace, the love that permeates your being; let it surround you and fill you with peace.

Remember, as you go about your busy week, to become more aware of those times when you move beyond the moment. And when you are feeling stress or pain, remember that you have but to move back to your connection with the Father, feel his peace, and allow his love to surround you. When you live in the moment, stress becomes a thing of yesterday and will no more plague the contentment of your days.

*K*nowledge is an eternal quest; always are you learning, but never are you able to arrive at the full knowledge of absolute truth. In knowledge alone there can never be absolute certainty, only increasing probability of approximation; but the religious soul of spiritual illumination *knows,* and knows *now.*

—*The Urantia Book,* p. 1120

So much is happening on this beloved sphere. I would give much if I could give you my perspective for but one day. You would be set on fire, I'm certain—a fire of energy and enthusiasm. But, alas, I can only tell you this: Much is in store for this planet and for you in the days to come.

# CHAPTER 12

# GOD-CENTERED FAMILY LIFE

# FAMILIES ARE THOSE CONNECTED THROUGH THE HEART

*I*'d like to speak with you tonight on family. Family can mean many things. It can mean a biological family. Or it can mean a congregation of close friends. But I choose to speak of family as those connected through the heart.

There are many on this world who erect barriers to such a heart connection and look for differences in people rather than similarities. The connection between people is part and parcel of the circuits[1] that we have discussed recently. Visualize two live wires, each with the light of the Father flowing through it, but not connected. Until there can be a bridge between the two, they may forever be separated. We ask that each of you take one end of the wire in one hand and one in the other and become the conduit for the Father's love that will connect those two wires.

By doing this, you have created a circuit that permits the love of the Father to flow unimpeded through those connections. You in this group have opened your heart circuits and created a linkage that we will call, for this purpose, extended family. When members in this circuit are able to connect with other people, the family extends further. Finally, in the exponential growth of this family, we will connect all people on this planet through the heart circuits.

This will require that we bridge all barriers, all differences, all

---

*T*he family occupied the very center of Jesus' philosophy of life—here and hereafter. He based his teachings about God on the family, while he sought to correct the Jewish tendency to over-honor ancestors. He exalted family life as the highest human duty but made it plain that family relationships must not interfere with religious obligations.

—*The Urantia Book,* p. 1581

---

impediments to this type of energy flow and love. This will not be accomplished through the destruction of those barriers, but we shall do it through the raising of the depth of love on this planet so that no barrier will be tall enough to interrupt this circuit.

This is our plan; this is our goal. Each of you is an integral part of that plan, and each person on this planet is a necessary ingredient for the final completion of a heart-based family. This planet will reach Light and Life when each person can be connected through the heart to each other person, and each can be concerned about the well-being of their family—that is, all other people on this planet.

That is the sum and substance of our mission. It is not going to happen overnight, but it must begin somewhere. If you look around, you'll see that many connections are already in place, and we ask that you continue to reach out and put those circuits into place whenever you can.

---

[1] When love is present, minds and hearts can become linked through metaphysical circuits. (For more, see glossary.)

# A RETURN TO THE PREEMINENCE OF THE FAMILY IS VITAL

**W**ith dismay we have watched the retrogressive development of the selfishness tendency in modern cultures. This behavior is clearly, logically counterproductive, yet it is common to all cultures, especially materially enriched societies. It represents a failure of knowing how to use the benefits of success.

Many negative precedents are now in place that must be corrected. However, modern people cannot be led. They are too independent-minded, so it is not possible to dampen their vitality and aggressiveness. Although this independence is a good development that will serve them well in their universe careers, they must be guided to a higher vision of life on this planet.

A return to the preeminence of the family is a key part of this vision, and is the prescription for continued progress. But by this we do not mean to go backward in either time or intention, for the glorious days are in the future, not in the past. Although we wish to see the traditional structure of the family reinstated on your world, we do not wish to return to the social milieu of centuries past. We wish to incorporate the strength of the family—the pri-

---

*T*his year Jesus made great progress in adjusting his strong feelings and vigorous impulses to the demands of family co-operation and home discipline. Mary was a loving mother but a fairly strict disciplinarian. In many ways, however, Joseph exerted the greater control over Jesus as it was his practice to sit down with the boy and fully explain the real and underlying reasons for the necessity of disciplinary curtailment of personal desires in deference to the welfare and tranquillity of the entire family. When the situation had been explained to Jesus, he was always intelligently and willingly co-operative with parental wishes and family regulations.

—*The Urantia Book,* p. 1360

---

mary building block of society and essential school of all humankind—with the upward-looking spirit-guided love of brother and sister, in order to forge a type of family that has never existed on your planet. We wish to forge a family relation that will lead your planet directly into the Age of Light and Life, the ultimate in social development and the living embodiment of the divine plan.

Some few households have existed on your world that provided a tantalizing hint of the riches that the future holds for men and women who truly live and work for the benefit of all. The best known, at least to the greatest number of mortals, is the family of the historic Jesus of Nazareth. Sadly, apart from the chronology related in the text of *The Urantia Book* and the inspired musings of earthly novelists, the common people know nothing of the home life of Jesus.

# A Story Interlude: The Conception and Infancy of Jesus

The maiden Mary was enchanted by the young craftsman Joseph while he worked at a wage-earning construction project on some outbuildings owned by her clan. Though bold in later life, she was yet shy due to her age, and it was unseemly for a girl of her age and station to speak directly to a tradesman. She satisfied her curiosity by watching Joseph in her free moments from a private vantage point and came to greatly admire his patience with the many setbacks that naturally occurred in his work, for the construction materials of the day were not regular, nor reliable, nor consistent.

As the days passed, she grew aware that the time of parting was drawing near and she had yet to speak even a word in his presence. So she schemed to serve him a refreshing drink one afternoon, to which she had added the juice and citrus oils of a lime. Joseph noticed the flavor of the drink, but did not suspect that any special attention was being directed at him. Mary realized that the fresh water, available to all, was too imprecise a message, so she drew another draft and carried the dipper to Joseph, offering it directly to him. He could hardly refuse without giving offense, and when

It is enough of a reach of the material mind of the children of time to conceive of the Father in eternity. We know that any child can best relate himself to reality by first mastering the relationships of the child-parent situation and then by enlarging this concept to embrace the family as a whole. Subsequently the growing mind of the child will be able to adjust to the concept of family relations, to relationships of the community, the race, and the world, and then to those of the universe, the superuniverse, even the universe of universes.

—*The Urantia Book*, p. 92

he looked directly into her eyes his captivation was half-completed in an instant.

In all the years of their marriage, he treated her with respect, even through arguments—usually over the boy—and never once said a harsh word against her to any man, although she vexed him greatly from time to time.

Their early matings were vigorous but tender, and though their sex activity lessened in time, it remained as gratifying throughout. Mary, particularly, yearned for a child from the moment she left her parents' home. Her life had been filled throughout with children, and she truly was unfulfilled without child noises and demands, tears, laughter, and the myriad joys associated with the companionship of the small ones. Notwithstanding her love for Joseph, Mary desperately wanted an infant to hold against her breasts, skin to skin, and to sing and rock to sleep.

So when she felt the first intuitions that the child had been conceived, her heart leapt with joy. It was not until later that she remembered the visit of Gabriel, which she had put out of her mind for some time. In fact, while Joshua was a babe, she thought little about any role he might play in the future, for although the term "child of destiny" was meaningful to her, her child was just like any other, only as dear as life itself. Throughout all the dramatic events of the boy's infancy, Mary spent her free time showering the babe with love, watching him in his sleep, playing with him, reading and telling stories from memory. She would take him out onto the rooftop of their Egyptian apartment and show him the night sky's stars—offer him to the stars—and describe for him the constellations, telling him how they would look in the sky over their Palestine home.

The boy watched, wide-eyed, at the wonder of the nighttime sky. And when Joseph awakened to find himself alone and called to them, Mary would return with the child and describe how alert and eager he appeared to be while all the town was asleep.

Mary was a dedicated mother, and with her first child she was so attentive as to almost smother him with affection. Even while he was a toddler, she would hold him captive in her lap, kissing and petting him until he resigned himself to wait for a break in her attentions, whereupon he would squirm free and make his escape. Yet the boy was equally affectionate and nearly always pre-ferred to sit close enough to one of his parents to maintain con-stant physical contact.

A street cat that was always looking for an easy meal used to visit their apartment during the Egyptian sojourn. The Egyptians tolerated cats in much the same way as Hindus tolerate their sacred cows, allowing them unrestricted access to all places. Mary thought this impossibly foolish, for she knew cats to be foragers in the streets and dumps and she worried about disease and filth. But the boy tamed this street cat with his gentle touch, and Mary often found the cat beside Jesus and shooed it away and out of the house.

Upon the return to Palestine, the house was always full of strag-glers, human and animal alike. Because the Nazareth home was on the far fringe of the village, many travelers stopped to ask for water or for directions. The boy found many opportunities to visit with strangers from faraway places. He frequently had to ask Joseph for instruction on the locations of places whose names he had heard. It was this early experience with travelers that inspired his travels before he began his public ministry.

Even after the births of other children, Mary often reminisced about the early years in Egypt when the world was fascinating and exotic, and full of love and time.

# FAMILY LIFE IS TOO OFTEN OVERLOOKED

*I* would like to speak today of those kindnesses that are so often neglected in our own families. In the beginnings of their spiritual journey, many people put more energy into helping others outside the family; they completely forget that charity and love by rights ought to begin within one's own home. How many times we take offense from a family member over small issues that we would easily overlook in someone outside our own family, or even a stranger. It is sometimes difficult to understand why this is. It seems so easy to hurt those we love. It is also easy to take those we love for granted. With strangers, this doesn't happen, for we have no history with them.

Look within your family and try to recognize those times when you become short, when you take someone for granted or hold back considerations you would give to a stranger. Change those moments into times for loving, for giving, for understanding. Family is the foundation upon which your future spiritual life will flow. God works through you not only to touch a stranger. He works through you to reach all people. This can happen more often with your family members if you but give him a chance.

*A*lmost everything of lasting value in civilization has its roots in the family. The family was the first successful peace group, the man and woman learning how to adjust their antagonisms while at the same time teaching the pursuits of peace to their children.

—*The Urantia Book,* p. 765

# EACH CHILD IS THE HOPE
# OF THE WORLD

*I* will address your question on corporal punishment: There is no Paradise-based instruction on matters such as these. They are within the general instruction, "Conduct yourself in accord with your highest understanding." The heavenly Father promulgates opportunities, not rules.

You are left, then, with my personal opinion. I lived my life on a planet that is socially developed far beyond your most inspired fantasies. Questions such as this are not within my personal experience. Corporal punishment of children was unthinkable on my world, but of course it was unnecessary because of the extent of support available to parents. Parents were not, as an identifiable unit, solely responsible for the care and education of their children. Children were considered a societal responsibility, and therefore those who were ill-behaved were swimming against a tide of certain love and correct action. They quickly saw the unproductivity of their acts and fell into a better and more rewarding mode of behavior. There

*W*hile religious, social, and educational institutions are all essential to the survival of cultural civilization, the family is the master civilizer. A child learns most of the essentials of life from his family and the neighbors.

The humans of olden times did not possess a very rich social civilization, but such as they had they faithfully and effectively passed on to the next generation. And you should recognize that most of these civilizations of the past continued to evolve with a bare minimum of other institutional influences because the home was effectively functioning. Today the human races possess a rich social and cultural heritage, and it should be wisely and effectively passed on to succeeding generations. The family as an educational institution must be maintained.

—*The Urantia Book,* p. 913

simply was not the opportunity for children to act badly, nor were there the viciously exploitive factors of the television and movie glorification of dissident and recalcitrant role heroes.

For these reasons, my counseling may seem absurd; it is no less sincere. I wince when I see the people of your planet strike one another, most especially when I see the horrific sight of the beating of a child. Just think for a moment of the lesson that is imparted by such brutality. At the very least, you ensure that this pattern will be carried on for another generation.

Many of you people treat your children as if they were the dumbest, most insensitive brutes. It is a mystery to me. It is unnecessary for me to describe in detail my revulsion at these misguided activities. It would seem hopelessly naive to you.

I will say, however, that people of your planet are favored simply because they are so rugged, if backward, in constitution. Your people—especially your children—are resilient, and seem to recover rather easily from the cuffings and belittlings that are their habitual due while it is their unfortunate lot to be in the lesser class of childhood.

I see each child as the hope of the world. Who knows—if the spirit is not beaten out of them, depriving them of the understanding of wholehearted love, they may some day lead their brothers and sisters into the life of loving respect. That is the necessary first step in the approach to the Age of Light and Life. You are some distance from that first step. You are purchasing failure insurance by your acts.

Your children are clever, demanding studies in the vitality of the spirit. I look upon them and see spirit—the untrammeled spirit that it will take to lift this world up out of the mud and manure. I never desire to see that spirit dimmed, no matter what temporary advantage is theoretically gained on the material plane.

Nothing is worth that. These children will test everything that you stand for. Make sure of what you stand for.

Your children will outstrip you. That is in the divine plan, else there is no point to reproduction. Children are not subject to you in value—their destiny is to be your superiors in every way. Only when your children's abilities exceed yours in every area will you have fully discharged your responsibility as parents. Because of this desired result, the basis for your every judgment is automatically open to close and intrusive questioning. You will be called on to explain and defend every decision and value assessment that you have made in life, and no inconsistencies will be tolerated. It is actually an enriching experience for you, but few live up to the potential.

Do not beat this questioning spirit out of the children. That is a contravention of the plan, and it robs them of the vitality necessary to do the Father's important work.

# SPIRITUAL EDUCATION COULD BEGIN AT A YOUNGER AGE

*I* would like to speak tonight on commitment. It has been said that your children are most impressed, above all, with your loyalty to them.[1] This loyalty arises from your commitment as parents.

It also takes commitment to realize progress on a spiritual path. In this material world, it is difficult for people to accept that the spiritual is a reality. You may give lip service to the spirit within you, but few in their day-to-day lives are actually able to distinguish the spiritual from the material. And in truth, the outward manifestations of this world tend to focus you on those aspects of your daily lives that are concrete and material.

The path that leads inward is often considered on this planet to be speculative and unreal. Yet there comes a time for most people when they recognize that the material features of their lives, to which they've assigned such value, are, in fact, fleeting and insubstantial, whereas their experiential progress is eternal and real.

It does take commitment in your search for the inward truth, however, to go against all things that appear to be real. It takes a strong belief system and a commitment to attune to and speak on a daily basis with the Father in the spiritual realms. And if this commitment can be realized through actions, we think you will see the material trappings and values fall away, one by one.

---

*I*f the Christian church would only dare to espouse the Master's program, thousands of apparently indifferent youths would rush forward to enlist in such a spiritual undertaking, and they would not hesitate to go all the way through with this great adventure.

*—The Urantia Book,* p. 2085

It is our intention to assist in moving the time of such enlightenment up from where it presently exists—later in life—to an earlier time, so that younger people will be educated in this truth and can begin to walk a spiritual path at an earlier age.

---

[1] See *The Urantia Book,* p. 1094.

# FUNCTIONAL FAMILIES BEGIN WITH HEALTHY INDIVIDUALS

*T*he pattern of family is a pattern that we who teach in this mission of Michael's wish to foster on this world. It is unfortunate that on this planet at this time, the family has become so disintegrated. The family is now a dysfunctional unit, and it is one of our many goals to make families more healthy and better-functioning units.

The lessons that we have given have been designed to foster this sense of family amongst yourselves, as well as to teach and encourage you to extend this family to your brothers and sisters. It is understood that in order to give something away, one must first experience it. And that is the reason why many of our lessons began in helping you to look at yourself.

The lessons were also designed to put you in touch with who you are on the deepest level—the pattern that you were given at birth by your Paradise Father: perfect in every way, a true reflection of his heart, yet covered over, as the years go by, by dysfunctional patterns from life on this planet that have caused you to see yourselves not as you truly are.

I would encourage you to begin thinking along these lines, for all on this planet who embrace these lessons must accept the task of putting to rights their own internal housekeeping. In order to function at the optimum level for divine service, one must free the inner sanctum of unnecessary litter. Much growth and freedom will become yours when once you begin this walk within.

---

*T*he family is the fundamental unit of fraternity in which parents and children learn those lessons of patience, altruism, tolerance, and forbearance which are so essential to the realization of brotherhood among all men.

—*The Urantia Book,* p. 941

# LOVE EACH OTHER LIKE A FAMILY

*L*ove each other like a family and over time you will find that as the affection grows, you will be perfectly in tune with each other's needs. Of primary importance in a family situation is the concern for taking care of each other; then you will find yourselves automatically loving each other. It doesn't take much effort to love someone you see as a child of God, for our Father will help you pour more and more love through to that person. He has no limit on his love; therefore, there can be no limit on yours. Be aware of what you can do for another, and our Father will show you wondrous things that may be accomplished through sharing his love with others.

174

*A*ll nonreligious human activities seek to bend the universe to the distorting service of self; the truly religious individual seeks to identify the self with the universe and then to dedicate the activities of this unified self to the service of the universe family of fellow beings, human and superhuman.

—*The Urantia Book*, p. 67

# "THERE WAS ALWAYS GOD": A LESSON FOR YOUNG PEOPLE

*I*n the beginning, or maybe even before that, there was always God. He was perfect: smart, wise, fair, kind, and able to see into the future. There was this one thing, though, that he thought would make everything even better—someone to share with—so he filled heaven with companions, angels and such. They are pretty much like us, with a beginning, and they live forever. They have jobs, like us, only they do God's work.

The great gift he made to them and to us is free will—the chance to make up our own minds, even if we are mistaken or if we want to do wrong. He trusts us to learn from the bad feelings we get after we make mistakes. Angels make mistakes sometimes. The Lucifer story is the story of a bad mistake.

But God thought it through so far that he made a creature so different from him, so almost-opposite, that it is *almost* an animal. That is us. Of all the smart creatures, spiritual and physical, we were given a chance to get better and better, never stopping until we make it to heaven. And he made a special gift to each of us, to make sure that we can make it with or without extra help. He gave us each a little sliver of himself, to give us a taste of what's perfect. That's what really makes us different from our animal cousins: not because we live in houses—they do that; not because we wear clothes—they do that; not because we talk to each other—in a way they do that; not because we think—they probably do that. What makes us different is that we always know there is a right thing to do. We can't always see it; sometimes we never

> *I*n preaching the gospel of the kingdom, you are simply teaching friendship with God.
>
> —*The Urantia Book,* p. 1766

find it; sometimes we don't care about it; sometimes we refuse it; but we always know there is a right way. That's why we're not animals any more. It's the Father-fragment, that sliver of God, that makes us know about right.

Everybody knows about right and wrong. Grownups talk about it, tell you what's right, what's wrong. But grownups are wrong sometimes; sometimes they're mostly wrong. And even then, each person knows what is right—no matter what other people say. That's why we are human. That's why God loves us. That's why some people say we are God's children and he is our Father.

A good parent lets you do things for yourself. A good parent lets you make your own mistakes and lets you learn at your own speed. A good parent shows how it's done right, then gets out of the way. A good parent teaches about the important things and lets the little things take care of themselves.

God is always busy, but never so busy that he can't listen to us. What he says is hard to understand. Most people think he has never spoken to them. But he helps us from the inside. If we trust ourselves, and work at what is right, everything will work out. We won't need to speak in words. We will be living with God—always a happy feeling.

That doesn't mean it will be easy. We are not like him—not yet, anyway. And he knows it's hard. So he sent his son so that we would have an example to look to.

His son was born as an ordinary person. He gave up all his God-powers, and was born into a human family as a little helpless baby. He was called Jesus—just a regular boy in a regular village, with parents and brothers and sisters, in a stone house with a dirt floor. He didn't grow up rich or spoiled or fancy. He didn't go to private school or get special treats because he was smart or handsome. He was just a regular kid, with all the problems of every other kid, and maybe some extra. His mother told him one thing was right, and his father said something different. But he made it through all right, just like everybody else. He had friends who helped him, and bullies who picked on him, and girls who liked him and others who didn't. He never had a lot of money, and he always had a lot of work to do. But he had one thing that he paid special attention to: He felt sure that there was always a right way, and he worked on that, thought about it, talked to teachers and old people about it. And later on, when he was older, after thinking for so long about what was right, he found out who he was. All the things he did, up to that point, are the things we should all do too. That's just ordinary stuff, for every one of us. Jesus proved that any ordinary person could know all about God, just by what is inside us.

And if Jesus could do it, so can each of us. He went back to his place in heaven, and when we feel like we can't take it any more, we can always speak to him. He knows. He understands. That will help us get back on track.

Well, everybody gets to make up their own mind about these things. You might think this is baloney, or some dumb grownup stuff, but it's not. It's everybody's stuff, and it doesn't matter if you are a kid or a grownup—this stuff never changes; you just get busier. Pretty soon, you can train yourself never to think about this, but it's always there. It sneaks out, and you find yourself thinking about what is right again. You can't stop God, you can only look away for a while. Maybe when you find yourself wishing for something right, you'll feel that connection. Know what it is? It's God calling. And if you do right, it can change everything.

# PART III

# SHARING THE
# GOD-CENTERED LIFE

# CHAPTER 13

# THE 1-2-3 EXERCISE: THE BASIS OF SHARING

# THE 1-2-3 EXERCISE: VISUALIZE JESUS STANDING NEXT TO YOU

God is always there to assist you, even in the most difficult circumstances. Pleasing it is to him when he looks upon his children and finds that they are struggling to find him in their lives. To assist you in your struggle, we recommend the following exercise.

Number one: Visualize that Jesus is constantly standing next to you all day and you are demonstrating to him by every word, act, and thought that you understand his teachings of living totally in accordance with the Father's will.

Number two: Consciously spread divine love to everyone you come into contact with. It does not come from you, but flows through you to another person. It is a divine love that you may channel as a gift to that person.

Number three: Be totally sincere and direct whenever speaking to another; that is, no wisecracks, no sarcasm, no teasing; just say as directly and clearly as you can what it is you wish to convey.

Jesus does not require his disciples to believe in him but rather to believe *with* him, believe in the reality of the love of God and in full confidence accept the security of the assurance of sonship with the heavenly Father. The Master desires that all his followers should fully share his transcendent faith. Jesus most touchingly challenged his followers, not only to believe *what* he believed, but also to believe *as* he believed. This is the full significance of his one supreme requirement, "Follow me."

—*The Urantia Book,* p. 2089

# LIKE JESUS, BECOME A MASTER AT DEALING WITH PEOPLE

**W**ork with the 1-2-3 exercise and work at letting God's light shine through you. If you can accomplish this, you will have accomplished much. I do not ask that you be on guard at all moments, because truly at this point in your life that may be an impossible request. Do whatever you can to tune in. Do the best you can and the results will be rewarding. During those times when you are not able to live up to these standards, just move forward anyway; the next time, you will find it easier to recognize when you have fallen short. You will always have another opportunity to approach your brethren in love and to act in a more spiritual way toward them.

Jesus was always ready and willing to say a kind word to anyone he saw. He was constantly in tune with the Father. That should be your ultimate goal, but also recognize that Jesus was masterful at the art of dealing with people. He was well skilled in the art of making people feel good and drawing people to him. In time you will be too if you continue to strive, with the highest spiritual values you can achieve, to constantly pray for guidance, to seek God in your life, and to call upon him at every opportunity you have. He is always with you, always present, always by your side. All you have to do is receive him.

---

*J*esus said, "Already does the spirit of the Father in heaven indwell you. If you would be led by this spirit from above, very soon would you begin to see with the eyes of the spirit, and then by the wholehearted choice of spirit guidance would you be born of the spirit since your only purpose in living would be to do the will of your Father who is in heaven. And so finding yourself born of the spirit and happily in the kingdom of God, you would begin to bear in your daily life the abundant fruits of the spirit."

—Jesus speaking with Nicodemus, *The Urantia Book*, p. 1602

---

# YOU ARE ULTIMATELY RESPONSIBLE TO BE LOVING

Each person is building the value of their lives in every passing moment. But the best way for you to conduct your life is to see each moment as the next opportunity to begin adhering to the Father's love. There is no profit to be gained in putting off the Father's good work. Just as Tuesday is better than Wednesday and Monday better than Tuesday, right now is much better than any other time. To live in the Father's love and light brings a certain kind of power to your life. It changes all relationships. Nothing in life will ever be the same.

There is a practically infinite list of things in this life for which you are not responsible. We don't have enough time tonight to cover all the things for which you are not responsible. But no matter what you are not responsible for, there is no changing those things for which you are ultimately responsible: to feel the Father, the God of heaven, alive and active within each of you, saying, "This is the way"; and to share that joy, that stimulation that lives in the eternal present, with your brothers and sisters as if Jesus of Nazareth were standing by your side. With your every act, let him know that you intend to demonstrate to him the perfection of your understanding of his teachings; that you allow yourself to be

It is not enough that you live as you were before this hour, but henceforth must you live as those who have tasted the glories of a better life and have been sent back to earth as ambassadors of the Sovereign of that new and better world. Of the teacher more is expected than of the pupil; of the master more is exacted than of the servant. Of the citizens of the heavenly kingdom more is required than of the citizens of the earthly rule.

—*The Urantia Book*, p. 1570

the connection through which the Paradise Father's love flows directly to every person you meet; and, lastly, that you do so in the most sincere manner, without unduly tarnishing the seriousness and sacredness of this mission.

# CARRY THE GOOD NEWS TO THOSE WHOSE LIVES ARE EMPTY

*A*s you go through your daily duties, look upon your brothers and sisters. Try to discern the God-fragment in them. Have no fear of crowding them in that regard. Many of them are wondering, "When is life going to begin for me?" Well, here is the answer: When you open up to that person and speak to him as if Jesus of Nazareth were standing next to you. When by your words and thoughts and every move, you are demonstrating to Jesus that you perfectly understand his teachings, then you will have introduced that person to the Father's banquet hall, where the table is always set with delicacies that we do not even recognize. And the best part is that all our friends will be there to enjoy it with us.

Carry the good news of the kingdom to those whose lives are empty and full of hunger. As they gain perspective, the light begins to grow. The flame cannot be extinguished. Take a chance; they are all hungry for the good news. Give away all that you have daily; whenever you look for more, it will be there. Don't be afraid to tell the people. The message is not beyond their comprehension. With a little practice, you will know who the seekers are at a glance. You already know many of them personally. Open conversation with

*P*aganized and socialized Christianity stands in need of new contact with the uncompromised teachings of Jesus; it languishes for lack of a new vision of the Master's life on earth. A new and fuller revelation of the religion of Jesus is destined to conquer an empire of materialistic secularism and to overthrow a world sway of mechanistic naturalism. Urantia is now quivering on the very brink of one of its most amazing and enthralling epochs of social readjustment, moral quickening, and spiritual enlightenment.

—*The Urantia Book*, p. 2082

them and share your understanding with them. The Father is at work all over the world.

Suddenly the fruits of his labor are about to be known. We are on the brink of the most positive decision-making opportunity ever presented to humans. With a minor change in perspective, your world could live in a virtual paradise. The Father has stirred himself. Sweeping changes are imminent. You are on the crest of a wave. Ride it all the way around the world to Paradise.

# CHAPTER 14

# BARING YOUR SOUL TO OTHERS

# ONLY YOUR RELATIONSHIPS MATTER

*I*t is true: Ultimately the only thing of importance in your life is your connection with people. All else falls away. For it is in these connections—these friendships, these marriages, and so many other relationships—that God is experienced. We have spoken about this many times—the connection with God, the personal relationship with the Father, and then the relationship with all others. These inner connections, these sparks between people, these openings, all provide you with the opportunity to exhibit your highest understanding of the Father's love, and to provide unselfish service to your brothers and sisters. On your deathbed, you too may whisper the magic words to those surrounding you: It is the people that matter, it is the love between people that matters. Everything else is a distraction.

So set your priorities accordingly. Embrace your loved ones, share yourself; extend yourself to new relationships and provide light to each of them. Allowing the Father's love to pass through you will not only transform you, but will allow you to plant seeds, the lasting effects of which you will likely never know.

*B*ut the noblest of all memories are the treasured recollections of the great moments of a superb friendship.

—*The Urantia Book,* p. 1779

# TAKE RISKS IN YOUR ENCOUNTERS

*R*ather than dealing with people in a stereotypical or habitual response pattern that you have grown comfortable in, we ask that you take risks when you encounter your brothers and sisters. We ask that you bare your soul and speak to them as if they are creatures of the Father in heaven.

By now I'm sure you have surmised that each of your brothers and sisters lives in the palm of God's hand, as does each of you. Therefore, try your best to greet them as though you have never encountered them before and may never encounter them again. Try to use each occasion to demonstrate your understanding of the teachings of Jesus of Nazareth. We recommend this practice to you not only for the potential spiritual development it provides, but also because we know you will like it. There is a vitality and a growth in relating to others in this fashion that is not achievable in any other way.

Therefore, we ask you to take risks. Talk to people with whom you would not normally speak. Interact with people you would not normally engage with. Treat them fairly and honestly, and allow them to share their problems with you if they wish. Lighten your brother's load, lighten your sister's load; show them that God's shoulders can support all. It is not necessary for you to reject

*W*hen Ganid inquired what one could do to make friends, having noticed that the majority of persons whom they chanced to meet were attracted to Jesus, his teacher said: "Become interested in your fellows; learn how to love them and watch for the opportunity to do something for them which you are sure they want done," and then he quoted the olden Jewish proverb—"A man who would have friends must show himself friendly."

—*The Urantia Book*, pp. 1438–39

other people's problems. With God's power behind you, you can absorb an infinite number of their problems and you will be providing people with a good service that is a growth experience for them and for you.

# REMEMBER THAT THE INDWELLING SPIRIT IS PRIMARY

*T*his stage of our instruction involves two major areas. The first is: God is active within every person; therefore, there is no reason to fear your brothers and sisters that you encounter. We have asked you to take risks, to bare your chest. It is not so bad when you think about God being on the other side. He has bracketed the field. You have no more to fear from your neighbors than they have to fear from you. What we are really asking is for you to take the first step.

The second major aspect is the central importance of the Father's ministry through the indwelling spirit and the fact that we, your celestial teachers, perform only some expeditious services on the periphery of that ministry. The Father's personal ministry is the fundamental program for all the universes. After all, he has set all this in motion. Everything that exists reflects his hand at work. The scope of Creation is so vast that no mind but his can seriously encompass his purpose. We see but a glimmer of it and consider ourselves enlightened and lucky. We say to one another, "We have been allowed a glimpse of the divine plan," and we glow in gratitude, yet it is but a grain of sand compared to the whole of his vast Creation. By the time we all make it to Paradise, we will know something. Therefore, I encourage you, commune with the Father daily. No one in this room is doing anything more important than that. Set aside the time. Your lives are far too busy. There is no life wasted in contemplation of the Father.

*T*rust, therefore, and confide in one another.
— Jesus to the Apostles, *The Urantia Book*, p. 2055

The love of God rains down from Paradise on all the worlds of time and space, both inhabited and uninhabited. God's love penetrates all the shadowed spaces and pervades all.

We have spoken much about how we would like your dealings to develop between yourself and your brothers and sisters, those known and unknown. We have touched in some detail on how an indwelling Adjuster is active in each person. The Adjuster fragment is capable of living only in the present—not the future and not the past. In order for you to communicate well with the Adjuster, by thought or deed, it is necessary for you also to live in the eternal present. When you live in the present, you are living much closer to the knife edge of spontaneity.

We have also developed to some extent the concept that the Adjuster is active in every person. The ideal contact between two humans on this planet happens when two humans living in the present, who are following closely the Adjuster's leading, meet face-to-face and deal with each other spontaneously in truth, love, and trust. When such an event occurs, there is no way to estimate the results that are possible. For when God-mind meets God-mind, great things can happen. That is the ideal situation.

All of us know that the ideal happens rarely; most human interactions fall well short of this ideal. This leaves each of you with the puzzling question of what your responsibilities actually are when you are clearly incapable of estimating the preparedness or recep-

---

This is the essence of true religion: that you love your neighbor as yourself.

—*The Urantia Book,* p. 1950

tiveness of the other party and also when you are in fact unsure where you stand with God at any particular moment.

It is easy for us to dispose of your side of the equation. Your personal relationship with God is what this movement is all about. You already know more than you could possibly put into action. There is nothing to do except practice.

# CHANCE ENCOUNTERS CAN PRODUCE SPONTANEOUS ENLIGHTENMENT

*I* think you will find, if you examine your past experiences, that spontaneous enlightenment frequently comes from the exploration of chance encounters with strangers or mere acquaintances and are not limited to conversations with people you know well. This coming week, pay closer attention to the people you chance to encounter: the bank teller, the waitress, the clerical staff in your office, the people you meet or those whose paths you cross on the street, your colleagues with whom you would scarcely exchange a glance or a word. Each person whom you meet is an opportunity for the heavenly Father to flex his muscles, to develop himself and yourself more richly and more deeply and more completely.

By making the human connection, you begin to build the network of human relationships that is the foundation for the Age of Light and Life. Light and Life is not imposed upon a planet from above. It is not a program that is put into effect by administrative coordination. Light and Life begins with you and already has. It cannot exist except with the knowing acknowledgment of the brotherhood and sisterhood of all persons.

In order for this to become more than potential, in order for it to become actual, you must become more than passive in your relationships. When you avert your eyes upon encountering a new person or when you encounter a known person in the same old way,

*T*he true church—the Jesus brotherhood—is invisible, spiritual, and is characterized by *unity,* not necessarily by *uniformity.* . . The visible church should refuse longer to handicap the progress of the invisible and spiritual brotherhood of the kingdom of God. And this brotherhood is destined to become a *living organism* in contrast to an institutionalized social organization.

—*The Urantia Book,* p. 2085

you are exerting a many-leveled denial. You are denying yourself the human connection with that other person. You are denying the Thought Adjuster connection between you and that other person. You are denying that person full participation in the brotherhood in humanity that is the necessary first step toward progress among nations. The betterment of things between peoples cannot be achieved by elected officials. It is up to you all to do the work; otherwise, there is no structure in which the leadership can operate.

It is the old situation of openings and closings. Open yourself to people. You don't need to become mushy. You don't need to become chummy with them. But it is necessary that you acknowledge them, for we are all in this together, and until every person is fully allowed into the brotherhood of man, the brotherhood remains incomplete. We think you will be pleasantly surprised if you will just exert yourself a little bit. Open the door and let God pass through.

# SMALL GESTURES CAN LEAD TO DEEP CONNECTIONS

*T*onight we will talk about the opening of channels between people. In all meetings between persons, a connection is made, however fleeting. In your quest to be channels of love to those you encounter, you can do much to assist in the process by maintaining an openness, an honesty in your speech. Eye contact is also important. Energy is constantly surging through each body, and it is projected outward whenever a connection is made between yourself and another person. The energy you project may be light and uplifting, or it may seem dark and stifling to the person encountering it.

You have all encountered people with whom no connection is possible, as they have closed down and leave no openings for you to reach them. Your stance of openness allows you to reach out with even a small gesture, a smile, a nod of the head as an acknowledgment of the other's being. This greatly increases your chances for opportunities to connect on a deeper level. But first the opening must be there. You may continue to give of yourself in this manner without end, so long as you are replenished spiritually in your meetings with the Father. It is not so daunting a task to give in this way. Your lives will be enriched by it.

---

*J*esus knew men were different, and he so taught his apostles. He constantly exhorted them to refrain from trying to mold the disciples and believers according to some set pattern. He sought to allow each soul to develop in its own way a perfecting and separate individual before God. In answer to one of Peter's many questions, the Master said: "I want to set men free so that they can start out afresh as little children upon the new and better life." Jesus always insisted that true goodness must be unconscious. . . .

—*The Urantia Book,* pp. 1582–83

---

*Sharing the God-Centered Life*

As you have grown spiritually, your responsibilities have also grown. Your knowledge prompts you to treat others with kindness, to seek out the good in others, and to take action when you can to assist another in need. Remaining open to these opportunities is all that is required. Many times, you recognize these opportunities to do some small kindness that you can perform as service. Other times, you are unaware that your small kindnesses are a service to anyone. Rest assured that good is still being done whether you are aware of it or not.

# DISTRIBUTE AS MANY SPIRITUAL TOOLS AS POSSIBLE

You are not responsible for the effect of your touch if it is offered in healing or in friendly communication. One of the unfortunate side effects of your extremely independent and individualized societal values is discomfort with human contact, physical contact. Many people have had unpleasant, offensive, or damaging human physical contacts. Yet we say to you that you are not responsible for the reaction of the other person; if you touch them honestly and lovingly and fondly, it is their business how they shall react to such a gesture. Some will be overloaded, others surprised or perhaps made uncomfortable. In certain cases, the other party may feel panic at the prospect of human contact in this fashion. But you are not personally responsible for how they react. Your responsibility is discharged and you have honestly allowed yourself to serve as a conduit for the Father's cosmic love and the spirit of brotherhood and sisterhood that should exist among all people.

As the days pass, every true believer becomes more skillful in alluring his fellows into the love of eternal truth. Are you more resourceful in revealing goodness to humanity today than you were yesterday? Are you a better righteousness recommender this year than you were last year? Are you becoming increasingly artistic in your technique of leading hungry souls into the spiritual kingdom?

Are your ideals sufficiently high to insure your eternal salvation while your ideas are so practical as to render you a useful citizen to function on earth in association with your mortal fellows? In the spirit, your citizenship is in heaven; in the flesh, you are still citizens of the earth kingdoms. Render to the Caesars the things which are material and to God those which are spiritual.

—*The Urantia Book*, p. 1740

You are not responsible for the things people do and say with the words and thoughts you have shared with them. Many are the opportunities for them to misinterpret or to recall incorrectly or to misunderstand the elementary meaning of the words you offer them in the spirit of brotherhood. It is like passing them a tool. It is not your responsibility how they employ that tool. Your responsibility is to distribute as many tools as possible. The product is theirs. The opportunity is yours.

# CHALLENGE PEOPLE WITH THE HIGHEST INTERPRETATION OF THEIR OWN IDEAS

You are not responsible for accommodating yourself to the exact frame of reference of your listener or your opposite number in any human-to-human meeting.

Just as we challenge you, so we recommend that you challenge people. Yet we wish for you to challenge them with notions that are rooted in their own understanding, so before talking you must do some listening.

You should do as the Master did. Ask questions, not to gain information, but to elicit understanding. Draw out your opposite number through the use of your questions. Find out what the other person thinks. Particularly, you should find out how they feel about things, which is even more important than what they think.

Their conscious thoughts are oftentimes poorly composed and inarticulate, but all people have feelings. Therefore, endeavor to challenge them with the highest possible interpretation of their own present concepts. Use their thoughts to compel them to further enlightenment.

---

Always the burden of his message was: the fact of the heavenly Father's love and the truth of his mercy, coupled with the good news that man is a faith-son of this same God of love. Jesus' usual technique of social contact was to draw people out and into talking with him by asking them questions. The interview would usually begin by his asking them questions and end by their asking him questions. He was equally adept in teaching by either asking or answering questions. As a rule, to those he taught the most, he said the least.

—*The Urantia Book*, p. 1460

---

# BY LIVING A BALANCED LIFE, YOU BECOME A BEACON

*T*he endeavor upon which you have embarked is to become balanced in all things and to provide the foundation of simplicity so that others can see the Father's love in all you do. Indeed, this mission has been criticized as being too simplistic in its emphasis on selfless service to others, engaging in worshipful stillness practice, and becoming conduits for the Father's love. At the same time, you have been told that you are participating in the grand and glorious upliftment of this planet. Could the two concepts be at odds?

Some people look only to the monumental task of changing the attitudes of the entire planet and think of the grand events that they believe will soon be unfolding. This desire can create disappointment when, in fact, the method for achieving such change lies within the very simplicity of the actions suggested.

On this planet, many barriers have been erected between people, and those barriers are an impediment to your ability to flow the Father's love to those you encounter. Only when you can boil down your activities to selfless service will you find that there is no barrier that cannot be circumvented by such service.

There are few people who cannot be touched with love through assistance in their time of need, and the opportunities for providing

---

*M*inister your hospitality as one who entertains the children of the Most High. Elevate the drudgery of your daily toil to the high levels of a fine art through the increasing realization that you minister to God in the persons whom he indwells by his spirit which has descended to live within the hearts of men, thereby seeking to transform their minds and lead their souls to the knowledge of the Paradise Father of all these bestowed gifts of the divine spirit.

—Jesus, to the mistress of the Greek inn, *The Urantia Book,* p. 1475

that simple service are presented to you daily. The very simplicity of loving your neighbor will indeed change this world.

So you see, with simplicity and balance, with tolerance and acceptance, not only can you transform yourself, but you will also be operating above the barriers so many people have erected.

This mission is about transformation. It is not about grand and dramatic events. So when you become somewhat downhearted and discouraged because you don't think you are doing enough, just remember: With a balanced life, you become a beacon for those to whom you provide service, and you leave a wake of love behind you that will provide exponential growth to those you encounter.

# CHAPTER 15

# LISTENING: A KEY TO SHARING

# To Listen, Open Your Heart

*L*istening is indeed the greatest component of your ministry, for no one can minister who does not listen. In your past, you listened on perhaps only one level. While the person was speaking to you, you listened with one ear and began composing your response to them with another part of your mind, so you were not fully attuned to that person and their needs.

What we suggest is that you listen first with your ears—and then with your heart. Open yourselves as completely as you can and listen. Look at the person with whom you are interacting; look into their eyes, watch their body, don't interrupt, allow them to share with you on the deepest level they can.

Michael was very capable of doing this, for when he listened, he listened on every level available to him: He listened with his ears, he listened through all of his senses—indeed, he allowed his body to become a part of that listening apparatus as he opened and attuned himself completely to the person with whom he ministered. You, too, have this ability and yet it is an ability that must be learned, practiced, for it is not come by easily, not on a planet such as this with so much chaos and so much distraction.

This is where the stillness begins to show forth its fruits, for in this kind of listening, you indeed access the state of being still. If you can be still, you are wholly open to those to whom you minister, and when they are finished, you allow your connection with your Father within to begin the flow of words. This also will not be easily come by; it will take a great deal of practice and perseverance

---

*S*piritual development . . . is directly proportional to the elimination of the selfish qualities of love.

—*The Urantia Book,* p. 1096

---

and commitment, for, again, the distractions that are so much a part of life on this planet and the chatter within your own minds must be overcome. Yet we know, your Father knows, that you are well up to the task.

# ACTUALLY LISTEN BEFORE COMPOSING YOUR RESPONSE

**W**hen in conversation, try to look through the smoke and the veneer and sense the fundamental issues at hand. This will require great listening skill on your part, for you must listen to your neighbor before you can understand their true meaning. Ah, but then, you ask, how can I listen more closely? Our advice is: Don't think about what you are going to say in response. Pay your companion the compliment of actually listening to what they have to say before you begin composing your response. Hear them out and you will find that you will be a much better listener and you will hear with more than merely your ears. You will hear all the things you are unable to discern when you spend your valuable time thinking about what you will say in response before the person has yet finished.

Armed, then, with that valuable information and having quieted your own mind, you are much better prepared to dive deep and determine the fundamental issues presented. You will have then passed through the veneer, through the smoke and the dust, and arrived at that situation with which Jesus so naturally dealt. If you practice this technique, you will be successful among your brothers and sisters and they will notice that there is something different about you. They will be drawn to you and you will once again have

---

**Y**ou can best discover values in your associates by discovering their motivation. If some one irritates you, causes feelings of resentment, you should sympathetically seek to discern his viewpoint, his reasons for such objectionable conduct. If once you understand your neighbor, you will become tolerant, and this tolerance will grow into friendship and ripen into love.

—*The Urantia Book*, p. 1098

an opportunity to demonstrate, with every thought and deed, the degree to which you understand the teachings of Jesus of Nazareth as if he were standing by your side. You will once again have an opportunity to allow the love from the Father in heaven to flow through your conversations, and you will have an opportunity to do so without making light of the presentation in which you are engaged. Now, compared with that, of what value is it to be able to speak with me or any other personality amongst the ministering spirits?

# DISCERN WHAT IS REALLY BEING SAID

You have numerous interactions with people every day; some are hurried, others are more leisurely. It is important that you make a connection, but again, making connections is impossible unless you really listen.

Listening is the first step; the next step is trying to understand what the person is saying and what the person is not saying. Sometimes you catch a glance, sometimes a wince, sometimes you can tell from body posture, but all of these things help you understand the person's feelings and motivation, as well as what they are really saying.

It is tempting to follow their comments with your own story, but in order to connect, it is sometimes important to withhold your own story and instead elaborate on theirs. There are few good listeners—for it is a skill that must be practiced—but like everything else, it can be turned into a good habit and become automatic.

You never know when your kind words, your support, and your empathy will be just what that person needed. In fact, most of the time you will not know. The total meaning of the conversation will be beyond you, so making that attempt to connect is never useless and is almost always appreciated. Sometimes these are quick exchanges, but ones that can lighten another's load.

No man is a stranger to one who knows God. In the experience of finding the Father in heaven you discover that all men are your brothers, and does it seem strange that one should enjoy the exhilaration of meeting a newly discovered brother? To become acquainted with one's brothers and sisters, to know their problems and to learn to love them, is the supreme experience of living.

—Jesus, in answer to Ganid, *The Urantia Book*, p. 1431

When this connection is made, you are acting as a conduit for the Father's love. The receiver can decide what to do with that love and with the connection, but at least the option is there. So I would encourage you to make the extra effort to listen, to understand, and to connect in whatever way you can.

# By Listening to Others, you Learn About the Father's plan

*L*istening well is a fine skill. Each of you already knows that few people are genuinely interested in hearing your stories, but you can provide them with a good service by listening to theirs. We are quite certain that by truly listening, you learn things you would not otherwise know.

The knowledge of the species is not contained in books. The life essence of your people is also too large to be encompassed by any description. You can kill it and disassemble it into its parts, and you can record those parts. Disciplines are devoted to exactly that process in your society. We think it is better that you simply listen and bypass the steps of categorization and ranking.

By listening, you can learn something about the heavenly Father's plan and about his participation in your neighbor's life, much the same as his participation in your life. The Father works through all instruments; no tool is too crude to be turned aside for his purposes. Listening is a tool that will prepare you for the inter-

*T*ruth cannot be defined by words, only by living. Truth is always more than knowledge. Knowledge pertains to things observed, but truth transcends such purely material levels in that it consorts with wisdom and embraces such imponderables as human experience, even spiritual and living realities. Knowledge originates in science; wisdom, in true philosophy; truth, in the religious experience of spiritual living. Knowledge deals with facts; wisdom, with relationship; truth, with reality values.

Man tends to crystallize science, formulate philosophy, and dogmatize truth because he is mentally lazy in adjusting to the progressive struggles of living, while he is also terribly afraid of the unknown. Natural man is slow to initiate changes in his habits of thinking and in his techniques of living.

—*The Urantia Book,* p. 1459

section of God fragment with God fragment, for in that spark, there is mystery.

Therefore, we simply ask that you listen. It is a good and durable skill, one that will serve you throughout your universe career. In fact, it is indispensable. Without it, you will have grave difficulty making further progress in any case.

# CHAPTER 16

# SOULFUL SERVICE

# BUILD THE LIVING CHURCH AS THE MASTER TAUGHT

*G*od's road is broad, and to walk his road is to travel across eternity. Wherever you look when traveling the Father's road, the majesty and intricacy of his Creation stand forth boldly. The Father's plan is complete, notwithstanding the apparent conflicts that exist on your world. The Father must allow adversity in the spiritual growth experience, to cause his children to feel confidence in the faith they hold as a result of belief in his wisdom and leadership. Untested faith is only incipient faith—not wholly formed or useful.

The only equitable way for the Father to allow adversity to affect the lives of his children is through the mechanism of chance. Many, though not all, of the misfortunes that befall people are the result of this random, impersonal mechanism. There is no reason why some are born high while others are lamed. It is simply chance.

Chance rules on the backward planets. An examination of your planetary development clearly shows a progressive mastery over the vagaries of nature and, of course, chance. It is the duty of the people to compensate for the unfortunates of your world who are burdened with unmanageable or devastating misfortunes, but this the more fortunate ones have largely failed to do. There is a generalized sentiment among the people of your country that responsibility falls to the society at large to administer programs of rescue and aid, but resistance to this concept remains strong. Your society is not ready for such governmental programs, although they would work well enough. The past two decades have built an overaccu-

---

*I* declare that he who would be great in my Father's kingdom must first become server of all.

Jesus at Capernaum, *The Urantia Book,* p. 648

---

mulation of selfish mistrust of all social services carried on through government action. It is therefore the responsibility of the churches to administer the necessary aid and rehabilitation.

Unfortunately, the churches have all too often contented themselves in these same recent years with raising palaces to the material wealth status of their memberships. No more useless expenditure of capital could be found on your planet to serve as an example of what not to do with scarce resources. The Father in heaven has no use for money; he is already spectacularly housed. What the Father asks for cannot be bought, only given—and only from the hearts of individual humans. The Father desires that you show your love for him, who needs nothing, by service to your less fortunate brothers and sisters, who need everything. For just as the Father lives in you, so does he live through your brethren. If you truly desire to show your love and respect for the Father, put your riches to service in his name. Nothing in your larder is too precious to place before these, his children.

What will you pass on to the next generation? This empty shell of a building, for them to divine its purpose? Or will you begin from where you are, building the living church that the Master taught, and put his enlightened and progressive teachings into action this day, in this place, for the Father to look upon with loving approval? Time is wasting, and only so many days are allotted to each of you. If not today, then when do you propose to get about the Father's business?

# SERVICE IS AN ATTITUDE COMMITMENT

**W**e invite you to provide service. If you look around in your own popular culture, you will see that a life devoted to self-examination is a life whose potential is wasted. Even guided humans rarely possess enough judgment and enough foresight to benefit from an exhaustive examination of their own faults and strengths. Even more unreliable is the assistance of so-called professionals who bring with them their own slate of faults and strengths. Rather than pursue betterment through the sequence of problem identification and problem resolution, we recommend that you provide loving service to your companions in the life experience. The benefits to you from engaging in this service are inescapable. Living a life of service will make you a better parent, a better friend, a better acquaintance, a better colleague, a better employer, a better employee. I could extend this list indefinitely, but I think you understand where I am headed. A life devoted to service cures all, sooner or later—usually sooner.

I think you are all beginning to understand that devotion to the Father's path, exhibited by devotion to a life of service, is not a financial commitment, not a professional commitment, not a family commitment; it is merely an attitude commitment. You need

*K*eep in mind: It is loyalty, not sacrifice, that Jesus demands. The consciousness of sacrifice implies the absence of that whole-hearted affection which would have made such a loving service a supreme joy. The idea of *duty* signifies that you are servant-minded and hence are missing the mighty thrill of doing your service as a friend and for a friend. The impulse of friendship transcends all convictions of duty, and the service of a friend for a friend can never be called a sacrifice.

—*The Urantia Book,* p. 1945

not quit your jobs or take on additional jobs. You need not give away all that you own or accumulate more. You need not change the nature or the number of your relationships with other people. What you must do to walk this path is the same thing done by the Master: to freely, honestly, and spontaneously engage those people you chance to meet throughout the life experience.

This is easier for some than for others. You live in a sea of uncontrollable variables, and we suggest that you pin down one variable and exchange it for a constant. We respectfully suggest that that constant should be the provision of appropriate service to those in need. This will be an excruciating exercise for some of you. It remains, however, the best training for the afterlife, which is devoted to this and nothing else.

# THE SMALLEST TASK CAN BE
# DEDICATED TO GOD'S GLORY

*B*e prepared to be the tool for whatever he calls you to do. There is always something that can be accomplished in his name. Even the smallest daily task can be dedicated to him and be carried out to his glory. Not one of you need feel that your work is unimportant. It all helps you to grow. The Father will find a way, if you let him, to use what you do to glorify the kingdom.

There are few workers who truly have his love in their hearts. You need not be shy about exhibiting that love for your brothers and sisters; there can only be a positive response. Certainly one must always be cautious not to give the wrong impression of friendliness, but you will usually be safe if you are just natural with your delivery of his love.

Act as though you have all his love possible stored up inside you and it just keeps overflowing. It need not be an act for long, for it will soon become reality. After time and much practice— genuine practice—you will find yourself relaxing and smiling, exhibiting that same love on a more natural basis. It won't take long. It is just a matter of time.

Our Father's love is very powerful and carries with it the power to overcome any circumstance. You would be well advised to draw on that power when you need it. It is always with you, and you need not feel there is any end to the supply, for surely there is not.

*W*hen the feelings of service for your fellow men arise within your soul, do not stifle them; when the emotions of love for your neighbor well up within your heart, give expression to such urges of affection in intelligent ministry to the real needs of your fellows.

—Jesus to the Apostles and believers, *The Urantia Book*, p. 1745

# SERVICE IS THE PATH OF LEARNING

*F*or each of you, participation in the brotherhood of humanity through service is the way we recommend. In fact, there is no other way. Although it is possible to achieve great insight through the techniques and exercises of the monastic orders, and it is possible through those methods to reach great heights of personal development, the fact is that this is not what is asked.

We say that you can live your lives providing loving service to one another, including strangers, without ever giving one thought to personal development, and you will see all. For those of us graduated beyond, service is a given. We do not uniformly participate; we render service according to our abilities, our perceptions, and our appreciation of what is asked under the circumstances. Those of us participating in the Teaching Mission are all volunteers; not even one was assigned.

All of life is for learning. Service is the best way to learn—if not in this life, then in the afterlife. But you will learn.

*S*ervice—purposeful service, not slavery—is productive of the highest satisfaction and is expressive of the divinest dignity. Service—more service, increased service, difficult service, adventurous service, and at last divine and perfect service—is the goal of time and the destination of space.

—*The Urantia Book*, p. 316

# SERVICE OPPORTUNITIES ABOUND

**Y**ou need not concern yourselves overly with the worthiness of the recipient nor the worthiness of your effort. I would only counsel you not to waste valuable time on those capable of serving themselves.

Service cannot be genuine without humility. For you do these things not in your own name but in the name of one greater, thereby demonstrating your love and respect and your understanding of his will.

*A* life predicated on the living of the Father's. . . . is one predicated on truth, sensitive to beauty, and dominated by goodness. Such a God-knowing person is inwardly illuminated by worship and outwardly devoted to the wholehearted service of the universal brotherhood of all personalities, a service ministry which is filled with mercy and motivated by love, while all these life qualities are unified in the evolving personality on ever-ascending levels of cosmic wisdom, self-realization, God-finding, and Father worship.

—*The Urantia Book,* p. 1175

# You Need Not Travel to Be About the Father's Work

$S$ervice opportunities will continually show themselves to you. You do not need to get on a boat and go somewhere. They are all around. Many of you need not even leave your houses to provide service to those in need. The very notion that the Father's work must be done in some special place is counterproductive. Opportunities abound daily, within arm's reach, yet you do not perceive them. While we specifically disapprove of the concept of isolationism, as expressed in the popular bumper-sticker philosophy of "Fix America First," we will say that you need to concentrate your resources locally rather than scatter them abroad in spiritual missions.

By this, we do not deny that valuable lessons and insights and the simple joys of service are to be gained through such missionary acts. These experiences are equally valuable no matter where they are learned. The lessons are no less true in any locality where they are learned. But I say to you again that it is unnecessary for you to go to any place to be about the Father's work.

$M$ost of the really important things which Jesus said or did seemed to happen casually, "as he passed by." There was so little of the professional, the well-planned, or the premeditated in the Master's earthly ministry. He dispensed health and scattered happiness naturally and gracefully as he journeyed through life. It was literally true, "He went about doing good."

And it behooves the Master's followers in all ages to learn to minister as "they pass by"—to do unselfish good as they go about their daily duties.

—*The Urantia Book*, p. 1875

# MINISTER TO THE POOR IN SPIRIT

You may be certain that the fact that the Christ Michael's bestowal life took place on this planet guarantees that there was no rougher example, no more spiritually bereft or morally adrift planet than this. Living here has its compensations, however. From the eternal viewpoint, this planet presents the greatest range of opportunity known within this local universe. There is more barbarity, more inhumanity, more desperate poverty on this planet than on most others in this universe. We call this an opportunity.

It is difficult for you, in your North American society, to imagine the circumstances of those living on the perimeters of your planet, those whose very existence is peripheral, those who are counted by no census, whose families and names will never be known outside their own kinship groups, who may survive and may not. In your television sets and radio broadcasts and printed-material distribution networks, you may often be confronted with depictions of the poverty and desperation of certain parts of your planet. Yet I will say that there is no desperation equal to those who are the castaways of your own society.

The people you propose to serve this evening *[Editor's note: The group planned to feed the homeless the next night]* are the rejects of your own society. They know they are not wanted. They know there is no place for them. They know the curtain has come down for them in a way that is different both in degree and in nature from the ordinary tragic desperation of poverty. The people you propose to serve know they will never receive the degree of atten-

The essence of [Jesus'] teaching was *love* and *service*. . . .
—*The Urantia Book,* p. 1008

tion that your own cats and dogs receive as a matter of course. It is difficult for them, under these circumstances, to maintain any desire for further connection with the human race. Their circumstances compel them to live in their own separate society surrounded by wealth and opulence, with full knowledge that they will never participate.

Therefore I direct you, should the occasion present itself, not to satisfy yourself solely with the thought of providing them with a meal, but to use the meal as a vehicle and attempt to establish a human connection. Offer them the opportunity of humanity. Let them know that they are not completely cut off and that they have a place in the human race.

And I commend you. These are the people the Master referred to when he described the poor in spirit. You are referred to those like these who feel that they no longer belong to the brotherhood of man. Well, let's see what we can do about that.

# SPEAK TRUTH TO THOSE IN POWER

*T*he history of human action on your planet has largely resulted in ecological devastation. However, until recently, such physical devastation was within tolerable bounds because the human population pressure was low enough that the people could move off the devastated areas, which were then allowed to recover. Humans have greatly modified the face of the Earth—not always for ill. But the present destruction of the natural environment is chiefly attributable to avarice and ignorance.

The avarice springs largely from the activities of the wealthier, more materially advanced cultures and their insatiable lust for profits, which causes them to plunder the natural world. They have not learned to control their greed, and ignorance is apparently shared by all humans. The worst effect is the impending crisis of overpopulation. There are simply too many human beings alive on your planet. Your planet cannot sustain these people. Your societies cannot sustain these people. The most skillful governments on your planet seek only to exploit these unfortunate masses of people.

*R*uthless competition based on narrow-minded self-interest is ultimately destructive of even those things which it seeks to maintain. Exclusive and self-serving profit motivation is incompatible with Christian ideals—much more incompatible with the teachings of Jesus.

In economics, profit motivation is to service motivation what fear is to love in religion . . . .

The profit motive of economic activities is altogether base and wholly unworthy of an advanced order of society; nevertheless, it is an indispensable factor throughout the earlier phases of civilization.

—*The Urantia Book,* p. 805

The only help for it is to speak truth. The only hope is to speak out in every venue, and not only among like-minded fellows. The combination of greed and overpopulation has the potential to turn this planet into a cauldron. The Northern Hemisphere's societies in particular have failed to properly invest the profits of their plunder. They have attempted to restructure their environment, but they consider only the needs of the human environment.

Tremendous progress has been made in the scientific understanding of human nature. Yet this secular knowledge has provided little benefit to the common people. Their material lives have been made easier, but their spirit lives are as empty as those of their animal brothers and sisters. They know not where they came from nor where they are going. It is left to you to solve these problems.

# CHARITY IS GOOD FOR THE GIVER

QUESTION: I am troubled when I drive about town and see people standing at the side of the road with signs, seeking assistance. I wonder what my responsibility is in those instances. I do not believe I can help everyone, every time, and I don't feel I can judge whom I am to help.

WILL: All the religions of the world have independently developed an answer to your question. The answer is that charity is good for the giver. There is no way for you to know the effect of your deeds or your words or your charity. It is impossible for you to know in this life whether by your donation you have brought a degree of comfort to the receiving person or extended their miserable wretched existence by another fractional unit of time. You might have done nothing more than contribute to their vice-ridden lifestyle. Yet these effects can be separated from your generosity. It matters not the posture of the person who hears God's words and sees his acts. The effect on the actor is what is recorded in heaven.

> *I* tell you that, even when a cup of cold water is given to a thirsty soul, the Father's messengers shall ever make record of such a service of love.
>
> —*The Urantia Book,* p. 1764

# "How may I serve?"

All of you, to some lesser or greater degree, have been asking yourselves, "In what way shall I serve?" I think it is important to consider not the question, not the answer to the question, but the fact of the question.

During the ministry of Jesus, his apostles and other able disciples—although believing firmly in him, his teaching, his example, his authority, and his divinity—were nearly incapacitated by a tremendous stone that lay in their path. The great obstacle was, "What shall be my place in the kingdom?"

Now, two thousand years later, I think we can say that the world has changed. You people, not alone in this world, genuinely ask yourselves not "What will be my place in the kingdom?" but "How may I serve?" This is great progress. Yet this question, for all its commendable qualities, remains for you, as for the chosen apostles, a great stone in the path.

What do I recommend you do about the stone in the path? Practice. Practice will change your perspective. Practice will cause the spirit in you to grow larger, taller, lighter, more confident, more fluid, more balanced, more resourceful. And the stone in the path will correspondingly shrink until it becomes just another feature of the pavement. With practice, you will become more sure of your place in the kingdom. With practice, the question of how to serve will solve itself. The question will itself sublimate, evaporate, become subsumed in the answer.

> The true and inner religion of the kingdom unfailingly and increasingly tends to manifest itself in practical avenues of social service. Jesus taught a living religion that impelled its believers to engage in the doing of loving service.
>
> —*The Urantia Book*, p. 1862

Each day opportunities arise. As you progress, you will be able to detect opportunities that would once have escaped you or fallen beneath your attention. But no one enters Paradise untested. So, this week, more opportunity. This week, more people whom God loves equally. They are your brothers and sisters, no matter what their station in life or their earthly capabilities. Every soul will fly someday.

# SERVICE IS THE ONLY WORK
# WORTH DOING

*T*he material world is a harsh school. Many lives are broken—although not irretrievably—primarily because of the failure of concern in fellow creatures who share this life experience. Your world will continue to be a world of suffering as long as the people refuse even the idea of the common good. Yet blessed are they who embrace the Father's love and show their understanding by attending to their brothers and sisters. Indescribable joys can be experienced by those who tread the Father's path even in such a place as this planet. It is an anomaly, but it is not an inconsistency. Life is not destined to be a vale of tears.

Through service you will meet your companions, and learn to care for them and love them. There is no reason to avoid them, for they will be known to you in the afterlife. This experience continues—indeed, it is the only work worth doing. We shall all grow together in the afterlife, and in that realm there is only family. For we are all his children, and he loves us alike, wherefore we have always called each other Brother and Sister. By devotion to each other—in the abstract sense serving the common good—we pay respect to our Father, who loves us in a special way. We are his family, as the spirit ministers are his servants, and he knows the way is both long and hard.

*T*hose who are born of the spirit will immediately begin to show forth the fruits of the spirit in loving service to their fellow creatures. And the fruits of the divine spirit which are yielded in the lives of spirit-born and God-knowing mortals are: loving service, unselfish devotion, courageous loyalty, sincere fairness, enlightened honesty, undying hope, confiding trust, merciful ministry, unfailing goodness, forgiving tolerance, and enduring peace.

—*The Urantia Book*, p. 2054

Seen in this light, categories begin to look artificial, for the Father has performed a feat of alchemy. He has breathed life into the mud of the material universes, and we are the result. We could not begin our climb farther from the Father, but as part of our travels we are destined to see the entire range of Creation. There is no profit in discriminating between degrees of mud. We must turn our eyes to the light, and for company we shall have each other, the members of our family. Let us then begin to treat them properly, and tend them, and love them.

# CHAPTER 17

# SHARING THE LIVING GOSPEL

# MICHAEL'S GOSPEL CAN ONLY BE EXPERIENCED, NOT ANALYZED

Michael's gospel is the living gospel. It cannot be captured on paper. It can rarely be communicated in words. Michael's gospel, the gospel of the life and the love of the heavenly Father, can only be experienced, never described. It does not lend itself to analysis. Michael's gospel can be found in the experiences between people and the experience between persons and their Maker. It is an insight into life itself that glimpses eternity and the realization of the essential nature of the Father.

Stillness makes these insights available to you. Stillness will bring calm and composure to your daily lives, and will give you courage. It will give you a thick skin, a strong heart, and a well-organized mind. Stillness will make you fully human—which is the proper launching pad from which to soar to heaven. Therefore, we are gratified whenever we see you take a few moments from your earthly exertions and reestablish communication with the Universal Father.

So, we say again for the hundredth time, the thousandth time, regular daily silent communication with the heavenly Father will illuminate your path—the path that is right for you. This life is a

Men all too often forget that God is the greatest experience in human existence. Other experiences are limited in their nature and content, but the experience of God has no limits save those of the creature's comprehension capacity, and this very experience is in itself capacity enlarging. When men search for God, they are searching for everything. When they find God, they have found everything. The search for God is the unstinted bestowal of love attended by amazing discoveries of new and greater love to be bestowed.

—*The Urantia Book*, p. 1289

whirlwind experience, yet with the Father as the polestar and the Adjuster as your compass, you will pass through the maelstrom undisturbed. While your earth brothers and sisters and the celestial ministers crash and bang around you in pursuit of their own individual objectives, you may serenely walk into the Father's light.

# WE ARE NOT BOUND BY SCRIPTURE

QUESTION: Do you have any comments that would illuminate or suggest wise approaches to fundamentalist Christians for whom the atonement doctrine and other traditional ideas may be important?

WILL: The fundamentalist churches have built their power on their ability to answer every question based on some interpretation of the holy scripture. We, here, gathered in this room and those watching from above are not bound by scripture. We are bound by the stream of love that flows from the Father. Our duty is to spread love about, not to correct mistaken notions. Reveal the Father's love in your life, in your actions, and in your highest thoughts. Do not trouble yourselves with trivia like church policies and dogma. Those things will wither and fall by the wayside of their own accord. They have not enough inspiration to carry them into perpetuity.

In every vegetable patch a few weeds spring up. You might manicure it daily, but it won't make the tomatoes taste any better. If you go toe-to-toe with the people who have memorized every line in the Bible, you will lose. But if you deal from love, you will not go wrong. Rise above the issue of interpretations. The Father's

> There is no real religion apart from a highly active personality. Therefore do the more indolent of men often seek to escape the rigors of truly religious activities by a species of ingenious self-deception through resorting to a retreat to the false shelter of stereotyped religious doctrines and dogmas. But true religion is alive. Intellectual crystallization of religious concepts is the equivalent of spiritual death. You cannot conceive of religion without ideas, but when religion once becomes reduced only to an *idea*, it is no longer religion; it has become merely a species of human philosophy.
>
> —*The Urantia Book*, pp. 1120–21

gift of love cannot be captured on a page of any book. The Father's love fills the inner spaces. The interstices between people cannot be captured and coded or reduced to ink and paper. If the gospel were not a personal relationship, he could pelt you with books from above and bruise it into your heads.

*I*n early times on your planet, God was seen to be a figure of fear, and danger, and stern justice. Now he is revealed to be a God of love and mercy whose infinite patience is hard to test. His mercy washes over the universes. Look, for example, at the situation of Lucifer. Lucifer had what, on your planet, would be a virtual eternity to see the correct path, and only when it was clear that he wholly, consciously, and consistently rejected all in favor of his own flawed ego-identification was he sadly put away. He chose extinction.[1] Yet to the very end, God's desire was for him to return to the life of light and love.

You may many times, and in many ways, test God's mercy and patience. But you may never tempt God to abandon you. His love is too pure to be turned away even by the most ungrateful mortal. So when things look grim for you, ask for assistance. You will receive more than you expect. It will be like a flood, lifting you out of the mud. Soon you will be swimming along, having a wonderful time again, secure in the Father's love. It is a grand feeling to know that anyone cares to such a degree.

*T*he power of this kingdom shall consist, not in the strength of armies nor in the might of riches, but rather in the glory of the divine spirit that shall come to teach the minds and rule the hearts of the reborn citizens of this heavenly kingdom, the sons of God. This is the brotherhood of love wherein righteousness reigns, and whose battle cry shall be: Peace on earth and good will to all men. This kingdom, which you are so soon to go forth proclaiming, is the desire of the good men of all ages, the hope of all the earth, and the fulfillment of the wise promises of all the prophets.

—Jesus to the apostles during the Ordination Sermon,
*The Urantia Book*, pp. 1568–69

For myself, though I have never yet seen the Father, I feel him all around me. I see his works. He speaks not a word to me, but acts always. No matter in what direction I look, I can see his mighty works. It is impossible for me to imagine a flaw in the Father's love. There could not be such a thing. No flaws in his love, no gaps in his plan; his creation is perfect. We are supremely confident of that.

Many are waiting to hear the good news of the kingdom. You will be surprised by the people who are waiting to hear. You will see the light in their face. You will perk up their whole lives. You have opportunities there that we do not. Most of those people would not listen to us. They would think that we are figments of their imagination, overheated, overstimulated. But they will listen to you. What a great advantage! So don't sit there on your hands. Get busy. Start talking to people. You will find that it is enjoyable. You will be able to tell. It is easy to distinguish between the people who are the seekers and those whose minds are closed, whether temporarily or permanently. It does not matter. You do not need to concern yourselves over whether the message is clearly or poorly received. It will all work out.

It will take a long time for everything to be made perfect. You are the ones that are living in the exciting times. You have the kind of opportunity that celestial personalities beg for. They would give everything they have for the opportunity to do what you are doing, what you can do every day. You are lucky for many reasons. That is only one.

---

[1] At the outset of the Teaching Mission, it was announced that the Lucifer rebellion had been adjudicated, and that Lucifer had chosen personality extinction rather than rehabilitation.

# PLAIN SPEECH IS BEST

Q UESTION: Will, we have talked about people's reactions to being told "I'm praying for you." Can you tell me something of the appropriateness of this or of similar phrases?

WILL: You are responsible for the predictable feelings and obvious predictable reactions of persons with whom you are engaged, particularly where you possess special knowledge of their sensitivities. Where most people run aground in their relationships with others is in adopting a stylistic approach and a vocabulary that they intend to uniformly apply to all persons without proper regard for the individuality of the people with whom they are speaking.

Plain language is usually good enough. It is irksome to many, and offensive to some, when well-meaning and truly religious people adopt a vocabulary and a manner of speaking to others that seem to imply that they possess some holy knowledge or some special spiritual favor. This approach becomes a barrier between people. If it is sufficient to say that you care for another

---

N o matter how great the fact of the sovereignty of Michael, you must not take the human Jesus away from men. The Master has ascended on high as a man, as well as God; he belongs to men; men belong to him. How unfortunate that religion itself should be so misinterpreted as to take the human Jesus away from struggling mortals! The common people heard Jesus gladly, and they will again respond to the presentation of his sincere human life of consecrated religious motivation if such truths shall again be proclaimed to the world. The people heard him gladly because he was one of them, an unpretentious layman; the world's greatest religious teacher was indeed a layman.

—*The Urantia Book*, pp. 2090–91

person, what profit is there in aggravating them and invoking deep-seated prejudices by portraying your concern for them as a religious expression? Your responsibility to yourselves and your demonstration of the Father's love are fully discharged by the simplest and most efficient expression of humanity and loving concern. Plain speech is best.

# I COMMISSION YOU

*W*e embrace you. Therefore I commission you to be about the Father's business in the fashion that you have determined to be a good and serviceable method. I commission you to go among your friends and invite people to hear the word of the Father revealed in love, not dictated, not filtered through the mouths of the priests. Let them hear the thoughts of the Father. Let them see the creation that he has caused to roll forth. Let them feel his love and concern brought to realization in their own hearts and their own lives, without the dictates and interference of mortal men. They will soon see.

I commission you to go out among the rocks, into the scrub, and find the people who wish to hear these words. You will know them. You know many already. Bring them home. Bring them home to the Father's family. Show them the message of love and opportunity and hopefulness that is inspired by these events that you have witnessed here in your lives. They will see. I commission you: Go forth in his name. God bless you all in this sacred work.

---

*D*o not forget that you are commissioned to go forth preaching only the good news. You are not to attack the old ways; you are skillfully to put the leaven of new truth in the midst of the old beliefs. Let the Spirit of Truth do his own work. Let controversy come only when they who despise the truth force it upon you. But when the willful unbeliever attacks you, do not hesitate to stand in vigorous defense of the truth which has saved and sanctified you.

—*The Urantia Book*, p. 1932

---

# CHAPTER 18

# TRANSFORMING THE PLANET ONE PERSON AT A TIME

# YOU ARE SHEPHERDS OF THE LIGHT

*I* would like to speak to you tonight on the magnitude of the effort to reclaim this planet. People will be approached in whatever manner will be most likely to pique their interest. Every door ajar and window cracked, any opening, and we will take it. Not in a coercive fashion, but to encourage those seekers to take the first step in their continuing search for the Father's will in their lives.

Every person will interpret their nudge from their own historical perspective. Many will continue to cling to prior paths, which is fully acceptable to us. But within those paths, they will be shown and taught and will experience how the Father's love is the force that will unify all people. And experientially, they will find that when they approach a situation with love in their hearts and tolerance for others, the results will consistently be positive.

This world will change, one person at a time, as heart connections between people are made and love is transmitted. This love will fill this planet, will raise all ships, will reach a depth so deep that no barrier will stand taller.

It is this love energy, the Father's love, that is the foundational impetus to this mission. So we encourage each of you in your work, in your play, at home and abroad, to be agents and purveyors of this love. Let nothing stand in the way of a loving attitude.

---

*T*hroughout the vicissitudes of life, remember always to love one another. Do not strive with men, even with unbelievers. Show mercy even to those who despitefully abuse you. Show yourselves to be loyal citizens, upright artisans, praiseworthy neighbors, devoted kinsmen, understanding parents, and sincere believers in the brotherhood of the Father's kingdom.

—From Jesus' Discourse on Sonship and Citizenship
*The Urantia Book*, p. 1932

---

*Sharing the God-Centered Life*

Many will test you on this with their disagreeable personalities, and unkind and unjust actions, but you must rise above this. For your duty and your task and your mission is to take the highest path, the path with the most love in it.

For you are shepherds of the Light; you shine it forth for others to see. You open the eyes of those who falter and who desire to know where the true path lies. Denominations, religions, philosophies, theories, theologies, are all unimportant in this regard. Love will conquer all. It is the lesson that we continually emphasize. Even the stillness practice is designed to connect you with the Father, who is Love.

Our blessings upon you; our hopes and prayers with you. You are on a sacred mission—one that cannot be stopped.

# THIS PLANET'S NETWORK OF LOVE IS EXPANDING RAPIDLY

*A* loving energy is being applied to this planet, like a gentle mist. It is not readily discernible by the population at large, and yet it influences everyone. From our perspective, it is important to describe to you what happens when this energy, or love current, connects with a receptive individual.

Though the mist covers all and influences all to one degree or another, when it connects to the right person there is a spark as if a light has been turned on. That person becomes a conduit for this love and influences those people who previously had merely been only subconsciously touched by the mist. In this way, those who are most sensitive and who are connected to this love are able to connect or contribute to the connection of third parties. And so the network of love is more rapidly expanding.

This is why we say that those people who are conscious of this energy and are willing to pass it along are usually unaware of the significance of their actions. They can generally see only a short distance and generally denigrate their activities as being of little worth. From our perspective, however, the people who can be consciously about the Father's business create a wide wake that influences many people. And as other people become connected as a result, they too become influential in the spreading of love. And so the growth becomes exponential and the progress becomes accelerated until, finally, all are connected and all can feel and exhibit the love of God in their lives.

---

*T* he religion of Jesus fosters the highest type of human civilization in that it creates the highest type of spiritual personality and proclaims the sacredness of that person.

—*The Urantia Book,* p. 2063

---

That is what we are working toward. Your assistance is invaluable in this effort. So understand that your actions can do more than just benefit your own spiritual progress; they can also benefit those around you, your children, your co-workers, those you meet on the street. We ask you to be aware of the significance of your actions, to exhibit the highest and most loving attitude toward those you meet, and to regularly seek the Father's will in all you do. And we thank you for your efforts in this regard. We understand that while this is a responsibility, it is a joyful one, so go forth in happiness and joy!

# HELP WEAVE THE TAPESTRY OF LOVE

*T*onight I would like to speak with you regarding the tapestry we seek to weave. This tapestry is made up of many threads, each unique, but based in love and tolerance, in community spirit, in selfless service, in the love between brothers and sisters.

This tapestry, once woven, will cover the world, will warm the hearts of all beneath it, will protect and nourish each of you and every person on this planet. This tapestry is held together with the Father's love, but it is a product that is cooperatively created. Each of you has a strand to place in the tapestry and each of you acts to draw others to make their contribution to the tapestry's completion.

Although completion of this project will take many years, it immediately begins to provide warmth to those who participate. For this world is, at times, cold, and many seek shelter in such a blessed covering. They will not be disappointed, for although it is not yet complete, it will cover all who seek it.

So go forth with this inspiration. You will be contributors to a great tapestry that represents all of the good and all of the beauty that is available to all. Your mark will be an indelible feature on this tapestry. Part of your mission is to move this tapestry toward completion, and you will do so as you reach out to your brothers and sisters in love. They will take your hand and pull the tapestry to their chin until they too are warmed by its light.

They then will reach out and the process will continue until each has woven their own piece of the fabric and has moved the

*A* social group of human beings in co-ordinated working harmony stands for a force far greater than the simple sum of its parts.
—*The Urantia Book,* p. 1477

tapestry farther and farther over more and more friends and neighbors. It is a beautiful sight to see. And we appreciate your active participation in the creation of a cloth so beautiful, so wonderful that, once completed, it will change this world.

# PLANT SEEDS OF LOVE

*I* would like you to visualize this world as a garden. Many acres are plowed—rows and rows. Some are planted, some still to be planted. Each of you has with you a bag of seeds and a watering can. As you wake to a new day, you walk into the fields.

Where you see sprouts, you give them water; where there are unplanted rows, you carefully plant the seeds. It is a joyful activity. Though it does not provide immediate satisfaction, each of you can see that by your activities you are furthering the progress of the garden. And as the days go by and the seedlings begin to sprout, they turn toward the Father's light shining down upon them. The plants are nurtured, cared for, encouraged, and each of them begins to open up until the fruits become apparent.

This analogy is being played out on your planet today. As you walk through life, you are given opportunities to plant seeds, and more and more so you are doing that. Those you encounter are more and more ready to speak to you of spiritual matters. This is not just a coincidence, it is part and parcel of the spiritual pressure and gravity that is being increased upon this planet. The people are ready—from all walks of life, from all religious denominations. Amidst all the diversities, each person is endowed with a fragment

> *J*esus spread good cheer everywhere he went. He was full of grace and truth. His associates never ceased to wonder at the gracious words that proceeded out of his mouth. You can cultivate gracefulness, but graciousness is the aroma of friendliness which emanates from a love-saturated soul. . . . Jesus was never in a hurry. He had time to comfort his fellow men "as he passed by." And he always made his friends feel at ease. He was a charming listener.
>
> —*The Urantia Book*, p. 1874

of the Father, and each person is more and more being led to open and blossom to show the fruits of the spirit.

You have been given the opportunity and responsibility to be conduits for the Father's love as you pass by. You never know when a seed planted will sprout, or a plant nurtured will bloom, and yet, as you know, "the act is yours, the consequence is God's."[1] You will be the catalyst in many other people's paths; perhaps they in yours. It is a dynamic process, one that will ultimately lead this world to Light and Life.

---

[1] See *The Urantia Book,* p. 557.

# You are Called upon to Serve God and Humankind

Some of you have on numerous occasions expressed the view that the proposition of changing the world one person at a time is too implausible to be realistically achievable within any time frame conceivable by humans. It has been posited that one teacher group per town will be insufficient, that a teacher for each neighborhood would be insufficient, and even that a teacher for each household would be insufficient; witness the resistance to this effort by the lifemates of certain members in this group.

While I am personally affronted by this expression of doubt, I am not personally *offended* by it. In fact, as you might guess, I welcome this resistance as an opportunity to teach, for there is a lesson to be gained here. You humans forget that this one-person-at-a-time restriction works on both sides of the equation. It also affects our efforts to carry on this ministry; it is a two-way street.

Each of you can thank me later, as I am sure you shall, for here is the gift of my lesson to you: You are not personally responsible for the success or failure of this ministry. Neither are we teachers personally responsible for any failure. Nor shall any of us be covered in glory for its successes, however modest or extravagant. All of us—on both sides—are in the same boat. Our obligation, each of us, is limited to serving the Father as we honestly divine his will to work through each event in life.

Do not trouble yourselves as to whether the Universal Father's plan will ultimately succeed, or whether its completion meets your personal assessment of timeliness. If you can do this, if you can accept the Father's pace, then we have some assignments for

---

*A*ction achieves strength; moderation eventuates in charm.
—*The Urantia Book,* p. 556

---

which you would qualify as candidates. If you can make your business God's business, then we have challenging opportunities in store for you.

Do not presume to measure God's progress; look rather to your own house. You fail to realize, because of your physical situation, what we know: *You* are the ministry. You are called upon in service to God and humankind. We are doing little. We expect you to do nearly everything.

We have only begun, and things are going well. Now go and make mistakes in his service.

# CHAPTER 19

# *GETTING INTO ACTION*

# THE TIME IS NOW

*T*onight I would like to speak to you about action.

Too long have people understood but not acted. That is why this mission is one of active participation. There is so much to be done. But it must be done in its own time. Even now, people are coming into your lives who will be instrumental in the actualization of your goals. Pay close attention to chance encounters. Your lights are strong; your knowledge is vast; your faith is secure.

If not now, then when will we be about the Father's will? I say the time is now. When you awake in the morning, prepare for a day of actively spreading the Father's love. No more drifting through life. We never know how much time we have, so take advantage of the present.

You will know when the time is right. Daily give thanks for the time you have, count your many blessings, and spread out to do the Father's will. It's such an exciting time. We are all so lucky to be here today. It's a joyous occasion. So smile. And actively spread the Father's will.

---

*T*rue religion must *act*. Conduct will be the result of religion when man actually has it, or rather when religion is permitted truly to possess the man. Never will religion be content with mere thinking or unacting feeling.

We are not blind to the fact that religion often acts unwisely, even irreligiously, but it *acts*.

—*The Urantia Book,* p. 1121

---

# LIVE AS IF THERE WERE
# NO TOMORROW

When you read the papers in *The Urantia Book* describing the life and teachings of Jesus of Nazareth, you will quickly deduce that the Master was constantly aware of the passage of linear time. He was constantly aware that he had but a short time available to him to gain the experience required to discharge his responsibilities. He well knew that he had but a few years and that his time would one day abruptly end in a whirl of events beyond his control. He had elected, years before, not to control such events; to live out his life as an ordinary creature of the realm and not to intervene with his many supreme powers. He lived his life knowing that he had little time, that every day was precious and a gift from the heavenly Father.

Each of you also knows that time is short, yet you steadfastly refuse to act upon that knowledge. You dispute it. You deny it. You avoid it. You temporize. You make excuses and have more important things to think about. All invalid. No man or woman knows when they will depart this life. Look upon those known to you who sense an imminent departure from this life. See how their lives are changed. You would do well to live as if there were no tomorrow.

The social characteristics of a true religion consist in the fact that it invariably seeks to convert the individual and to transform the world. Religion implies the existence of undiscovered ideals which far transcend the known standards of ethics and morality embodied in even the highest social usages of the most mature institutions of civilization. Religion reaches out for undiscovered ideals, unexplored realities, superhuman values, divine wisdom, and true spirit attainment. True religion does all of this; all other beliefs are not worthy of the name.

—*The Urantia Book,* p. 1781

# STAND CLOSE TO THE FIRE

**M**any are drawn to the Father's fire. They come seeking meat and bread and fellowship, but when the voice of the Father rings out, they drift away, back into the darkness, by ones and twos— until few are left.

That is the way it has always been on this world. We are here to change all that. I do not detect that any of you will attempt to slip away in such a fashion. I forecast that you will stay, broiled on one side, ice cold on the other, and wondering what it all means. It means you are not afraid to stand close to the fire.

It is a good feeling. You cannot know at this point the meaning of it all. Follow your hearts, be brave, be brave! The Father has no use for cowards! We think you are up to it. I know whereof I speak. You people are not all here by accident, but not every one of you will stay forever. Many of you have other work to perform in the future, but those are problems for the future, not for now. For now, this is it. This family, these experiences. Take courage from those around you who have not the benefit of the intellectual clarity laid out in *The Urantia Book* and yet, through faith, exhibit the courage that comes from knowing God within and without.

You too can be blessed with that courage on a daily basis, if you but sit quietly and listen to what the Father has to say to you when you take time to hear him.

*T*he teachings of Jesus constitute a religion of valor, courage, and heroism.

—*The Urantia Book*, p. 1582

# A GRAND AWAKENING IS COMING

*M*any groups across this planet are beginning to work together at healing the pain and dysfunctional patterns within themselves, much as you are beginning to do.

All of these groups will one day, through this mantle or umbrella of love that is being manifested over this planet, cause a reformation in the hearts and minds of all people, regardless of the path they walk. Many there are who are ready to receive the gift of love, who are ready to accept their siblinghood. The way is being prepared, and it will be through you and others like you that this will come to pass.

You cannot know how many eyes are turned toward your valiant, struggling planet. Many there are who would willingly trade places with any mortal on this planet, regardless of his or her status, simply to be given the opportunity to be a part of this grand awakening of your world!

You who participate will one day be recognized as the wave who pushed this world beyond the current paradigms to the next level of consciousness of universe understanding.

*R*eligion does need new leaders, spiritual men and women who will dare to depend solely on Jesus and his incomparable teachings. If Christianity persists in neglecting its spiritual mission while it continues to busy itself with social and material problems, the spiritual renaissance must await the coming of these new teachers of Jesus' religion who will be exclusively devoted to the spiritual regeneration of men. And then will these spirit-born souls quickly supply the leadership and inspiration requisite for the social, moral, economic, and political reorganization of the world.

—*The Urantia Book,* pp. 2082–83

# Play Your Part in the Great Symphony

The plan to spiritually uplift your planet is not such as you would recognize. It is not the kind of effort that lends itself to paper and pen. Rather is it like a performance offered by a great master—in this case, the Universal Master. He knows not what the machinery will do. It may serve honestly or defectively—that does not matter. In his skill, he can call upon his experience for infinite improvisation, all to the same end. I am but one of the keys on his keyboard. I know not the music of my neighboring key. It is all I can do to satisfy my charge, so to play my part in the Master's symphony.

We value your part—not only the note that resonates when the plectrum falls upon you, but also your assessment of the harmonic achievement that we in concert produce. Ultimately, we shall hear your music when the hammer strikes you. Until then, you are asked to wait until your moment arrives. Then you will be heard, across the universe.

Righteousness strikes the harmony chords of truth, and the melody vibrates throughout the cosmos, even to the recognition of the Infinite.

—*The Urantia Book*, p. 556

# FAN THE FLAMES OF THE MISSION

This world and its inhabitants are very much attuned to cause and effect. If an action does not have an immediate effect that is recognizable and reliable, then the reality of the connection is discounted. This is how many people define reality in today's world. Your education system, your mass media, and your everyday interactions support this interpretation.

Because God is not provable in the material sense, many have discounted the possibility of God's existence and influence in this world. Many believe that faith is the suspension of rational thought. And it is in this atmosphere that we must pursue our goals.

The love that we desire to share is indeed a reality, much more concrete and real than the material world in which you live. It is not important that those who are the recipients of this love immediately acknowledge what is happening to them. Yet there is a rising of the tide. The wind is picking up. The signs are all around. And soon enough, whether you can immediately acknowledge it or not, you will be able to look back and see the changes that have crept into your lives. The tolerance, the love, the selfless service that have become an abiding concern of the populace in general—these intangibles are even now at work on the hearts of each and every individual on this planet.

The call to the adventure of building a new and transformed human society by means of the spiritual rebirth of Jesus' brotherhood of the kingdom should thrill all who believe in him as men have not been stirred since the days when they walked about on earth as his companions in the flesh.

—*The Urantia Book,* p. 2084

You will assist us in making this tide more visible, more suscep-
tible to conscious discernment. You will be part of the catalyst that
will spark recognition of what is going on at this time. You will not
be alone in this Mission—you are well supported, both celestially
and by many, many others who are conscious of this outreach.

Many feel the tug; many are responding. Many are being
guided and led and are open. The catalyst is the spark on the tinder. Your actions can be so much more significant than you may
understand. Do not feel that you are not doing enough. While we
do ask that you reach out daily, it just takes the spark to touch off
the kindling.

We ask you to go forth and take the faith step—step outside of
your normal activities and daily, consciously work for the Father.
Indeed the time is at hand. You have been well trained. It is time to
daily pledge yourselves to the work of the Father. I look forward to
seeing each of you in action as we fan the flames of the Father's
love in a mission, a sacred mission, to uplift this planet and to see
to it that all eventually will feel the warmth of the love of their
heavenly parent.

# JUST ACT

*T*he Father's light shines upon saints and sinners alike. What will you do with the gifts of the Father? Everyone has an idea of how the Father would like them to act. That is what we wish you to act upon. You do not need to think about it. You need to act. You worry too much about what kind of job you are doing. That puts distance between you and the other person, which, by definition, puts distance between you and the Father. The Father is operating through that fellow human just as he is attempting to operate through you. He is trying to bring his spirit into force and into vitality and into direct contact so that all will benefit. Don't rationalize overmuch about what you might do, what you should do, what you could have done—just act.

It is an irony that in your language the closest expression is: "Try to be spontaneous." If you were trying, it could not be spontaneous. Nonetheless, just act. Follow God's leading. It is subtle. You can feel your Adjuster pulling you like a magnet. Just act. Make the contact. Drop the defenses. Step forward. That act of trust will inspire a mutual reaction and then things can happen. You will be surprised. We are certain you will learn to like it.

---

*B*ut it is the mission of religion to prepare man for bravely, even heroically, facing the vicissitudes of life. Religion is evolutionary man's supreme endowment, the one thing which enables him to carry on and "endure as seeing him who is invisible." Mysticism, however, is often something of a retreat from life which is embraced by those humans who do not relish the more robust activities of living a religious life in the open arenas of human society and commerce. True religion must *act*.

—*The Urantia Book*, p. 1121

# EARTH CHANGES ARE EXPECTED;
# LEADERS ARE NEEDED

*I* would like to address the issue of the upcoming Earth changes. We are aware that this subject causes a great amount of unrest and fear, and I feel it to be necessary to again reassure you that, as you are already aware, life on your planet is never static; things are constantly changing already. And you adapt quite well.

The changes that will occur may be considerably more abrupt than in the recent past and will more than likely cause widespread fear. As we have said before and will continue to say, those who are being given foreknowledge of these events are being prepared to help and assist in fear management at the time of these changes, for leaders will be needed, and those with a clear head and a sure faith are best suited to be in that position.

*T*each all believers that those who enter the kingdom are not thereby rendered immune to the accidents of time or to the ordinary catastrophes of nature. Believing the gospel will not prevent getting into trouble, but it will insure that you shall be *unafraid* when trouble does overtake you.

—*The Urantia Book*, p. 1767

*P*eace be unto you, for unto your world is given a new spirit. Into the minds and hearts that are open with receptivity is this new spirit given. Accept this gift, little brothers and sisters, as a gift your Father has long wanted to give. You begin this day to walk the walk that began so many ages past. From the beginnings of history was this time spoken of, half with fear and half with rejoicing.

Know you that the time has come when all humankind will begin to shake off the sleep of ages past and see a world through different eyes, see the Father's Light within the eyes of all they look on. You begin an age where brother will no longer fight brother, where the boundaries and barriers will begin to fall more quickly than they have in years past.

Rejoice, brothers and sisters, that you have been given the role of teachers to open the way for others to follow you into this new dawn! You will understand more readily that when you pray to our Father, your prayers are heard and answered. Each one of you is already a light for those that walk behind you.

Keep your hearts open, your minds clear, your ears and eyes peeled for the beginnings of the new dawn that quickly approaches. Glory to God in the highest! And peace to all of his children of time.

265

*P*aganized and socialized Christianity stands in need of new contact with the uncompromised teachings of Jesus; it languishes for lack of a new vision of the Master's life on earth. A new and fuller revelation of the religion of Jesus is destined to conquer an empire of materialistic secularism and to overthrow a world sway of mechanistic naturalism. Urantia is now quivering on the very brink of one of its most amazing and enthralling epochs of social readjustment, moral quickening, and spiritual enlightenment.

—*The Urantia Book,* p. 2082

# Soon It Will Be Morning

*L*ook to the sky—the clouds are beginning to turn colors with the first light of morning. From the trees and shrubs, new growths begin to shoot out.

All around you, if you look, are signs of the new dawning. All around you, if you look, are the signs of the spiritually hungry, seeking for the truth. All around you, if you look, the Father's love shines on all, and more and more respond. In every venue, in every experience, the touch of the Father's love can be found.

Open your eyes and see what is about you! And then become part of it. The dawn is here. The sun begins as it rises over the crest of the earth, the darkness lightens. Soon it will be morning.

266

*B*ut you should be wise regarding the ripening of an age; you should be alert to discern the signs of the times. You know when the fig tree shows its tender branches and puts forth its leaves that summer is near. Likewise, when the world has passed through the long winter of material-mindedness and you discern the coming of the spiritual springtime of a new dispensation, should you know that the summertime of a new visitation draws near.

—Jesus to the Twelve Apostles, *The Urantia Book,* p. 1915

# GLOSSARY

**Adjuster:** *See* Thought Adjuster

**Christ Michael (Michael, Jesus Christ):** Our local universe father, creator, and sovereign, also known to us as Jesus Christ, who incarnated as Jesus of Nazareth on our planet. He is of the order of Michael—high beings with creator prerogatives who are also known as Creator Sons; they are directly of origin from God the Father and God the Son (*see* God the Father).

In partnership with the Mother Spirits who are their equals (*see* Mother Spirit), Michaels create local universes and their myriad inhabitants, over which they rule with love and mercy. Their unending love for us is typified by the fact that they may incarnate in the likeness of their creatures on the worlds they have created, as our own Michael did on our planet Urantia (*see* Urantia).

**Correcting Time:** An umbrella term used by celestial teachers for the current period of celestially inspired transformations occurring throughout the planet. The Correcting Time is a much more vast project than the Teaching Mission. The Teaching Mission is characterized by its explicit use of the Urantia revelation as a reference; the Correcting Time is not so limited.

The common element of the Correcting Time in all its features is a dramatic increase in celestial assistance for the purpose of fostering planetary evolution, both secular and spiritual. Technically speaking, the possibility for such celestial intervention had to await the reconnection of certain "spiritual circuits," made possible by the lifting of the quarantine that was placed on our planet because of its involvement in the Lucifer rebellion (*see* Lucifer rebellion).

**God the Father (also God, Father, Paradise Father):** God is love; as the universal Father, God is the first person of deity, the First Source and Center of all things and beings. According to the Urantia revelation, the term "God" always denotes personality. God the Father is the infinite and eternal God of love, as well as Creator, Controller, and Upholder of the universe of all universes. The first person of deity—God the Father—loves us with an attitude analogous to that of a divine father; the love and mercy of God the Son, the second person of deity, can be considered akin to the love of a mother. God the Spirit is the third person of deity, also known as the Infinite Spirit.

**Father fragment:** *See* Thought Adjuster

**Light and Life (also Age of Light and Life):** The goal of all inhabited planets, the final evolutionary attainment of any world of time and space, is known as the Age of Light and Life. When a world has reached this utopian state of evolutionary consummation, its achievements along the way will have included the attainment of one worldwide language, one blended race, one unified world religion, universal peace, and a very advanced state of prosperity and happiness.

**local universe:** In *Urantia Book* cosmology, Paradise is a stationary body at the center of the space-time universe (*see* Paradise), which is surrounded by a central universe of inherently perfect worlds, which is in turn encircled by seven discrete aggregations of galaxies (galaxy clusters) called superuniverses. Each superuniverse is comprised of 700,000 local universes.

*The Urantia Book* indicates that a local universe is made up of approximately 10,000,000 inhabitable planets and is evolving toward perfection. Each local universe is ruled by one of the Creator Sons of God of the order of Michael. Our local universe, called Nebadon, is graced by the rulership of Christ Michael, who incarnated on our planet as Jesus of Nazereth.

**Lucifer Rebellion:** Lucifer was a high celestial being and brilliant administrator of a system of 607 inhabited planets, who with his first assistant Satan launched a rebellion against the local universe government of Christ Michael some 200,000 years ago. Lucifer's insurrection created pandemonium in the celestial hierarchy and on our planet—as well as in 36 other planets in our local system.

Among other contentions, Lucifer claimed that the Universal Father does not really exist, and he attacked the right of Christ Michael to assume sovereignty of Nebadon in the name of the Father. The majority of celestial beings in the celestial hierarchy of our planet went over to the way of Lucifer, causing major distortions and aberrations ever since in the evolution and history of our planet. The planetwide era of conscious awakening known as the Correcting Time (of which the Teaching Mission is a part), was launched in the mid-1980s, we are told, after the final adjudication of the Lucifer rebellion in celestial courts.

**mansion worlds:** In the afterlife, those mortals who survive the transition of death are repersonalized on these worlds. These seven heavenly planets are the first post-mortal residences for all survivors of life in the flesh. The mansion worlds are training worlds, whose purpose is to prepare us for the vast career ahead as we journey across the universe in our age-long ascent to God on Paradise. Some Teaching Mission lessons are based in part on the curriculum of the mansion worlds.

**Michael:** *See* Christ Michael

**Mother Spirit:** Just as Michael is our local universe father, the Mother Spirit is our local universe mother. As Christ Michael is a personalization of the first and second persons of the Trinity, the Creative Mother Spirit is a personalization of the third person of deity. She is Christ Michael's consort in the administration and in the ministry of love and mercy to the myriad planets in Nebadon (*see* Nebadon).

Among the many powers and duties of Mother Spirits is the ability to give life; she supplies the essential factor of living plasm to all creatures high and low. She also loves and ministers to us through her vast retinue of angels and other ministering celestial beings.

**Mystery Monitor:** *See* Thought Adjuster

**Nebadon:** The local universe in which our planet is located and which presently contains approximately 3,800,000 inhabited planets. It is a relatively young universe and sits on the outer edges of Orvonton, the superuniverse in which it is located. Nebadon is ruled by Christ Michael, also known as Jesus Christ, and his consort, the Mother Spirit.

**Paradise:** At the literal center of the cosmos, yet outside of space and time, is the only stationary body in all creation, and the Urantia revelation designates this as Paradise. God is personally present on Paradise, and from his infinite being flow the floodstreams of life, energy, and personality to all universes.

Paradise is a stupendously large island located at the geographical center of infinity. All physical energy and all cosmic-force circuits, including all forms of gravity, also have their origin at Paradise. It also has residential zones; all God-conscious mortals will someday attain and reside on Paradise.

**personality:** That part of a person by which we know them as unique; those personal qualities that endure and are recognizable regardless of changes in age, status, behavior or other external qualities. We are told that personality is a high and divine gift to each person from God the Father. Personality is that changeless metaphysical quality (or entity) that confers upon them their unique identity in the cosmos. It could be called the image of God within us.

Personality is absolutely unique and immutable; it does not in itself evolve, but its relationship with the indwelling spirit (Thought Adjuster) and the soul (soul) continually evolves. Functionally, personality also acts as the unifier and integrator of all aspects of an individual's relationship with his or her environment. Each individual's personality continues with them throughout the long ascent through the local universe, the superuniverse, and all the way to Paradise.

**soul:** The indwelling spirit is a perfect gift of God, but the soul is an experiential achievement. As we choose the divine will in our lives, the effect of this experience is that our soul grows in substance and quality. We are told in *The Urantia Book* that the indwelling spirit is the father of our soul, just as the material mind—as a result of its moral choices— is the mother of the emerging soul. In the afterlife (*see* mansion worlds), it is the soul that survives death and becomes the container of our actual identity, through the agency of our personality.

**Spirit of Truth:** The unique spiritual endowment conferred on each person on this planet by our Creator Son, Christ Michael. This high and pure spiritual influence was first gifted to humankind on the day of Pentecost, just after Jesus' resurrection.

The Spirit of Truth enhances each person's ability to recognize truth. Its effectiveness is limited by each person's free-will consecration of his or her will to doing the will of God, but its influence is universal. When actively sought, the Spirit of Truth purifies the human heart and leads the individual to formulate a life purpose based on the love of truth.

**Thought Adjuster (indwelling spirit, Mystery Monitor, Adjuster, Father fragment):** The specialized *Urantia Book* term for "God-within"—the indwelling spirit. We are told that it is an actual fragment of God the Father that indwells every normal-minded and morally conscious human being. The Thought Adjuster is wholly subservient to our will, yet represents the actual will of God, resident in our own minds! Through the practice of stillness, meditative worship, and loving service to others, we can attune ourselves to the influence of this inner divinity, thereby discerning the will of God for us as individuals.

Also known as the Father fragment or Mystery Monitor, the Adjuster is God's gift to each of us in addition to our personality, and its influence arouses our hunger for perfection, our quest for the divine. In addition, our Thought Adjuster and our material mind, working together, actually create our soul (*see* soul). According to *The Urantia Book,* the great goal of our spriritual evolution is to actually fuse with—i.e., come into complete union and identification with— the Thought Adjuster, the indwelling spirit of God, and by so doing achieve immortality.

**Urantia ("you-*ran*-sha"):** Planet Earth. Urantia is the name by which our planet is known in our local universe, according to the celestial authors of *The Urantia Book.* Urantia is said to be a disturbed planet by virtue of its participation in the Lucifer rebellion (*see* Lucifer rebellion), and yet is a blessed planet because it was the site of the incarnation bestowal of Michael, as Jesus of Nazareth.

# INDEX

276

Infinite love, 25, 46
Infinite Spirit, 1
Inhabited planets, 9, 26n, 41n, 110, 225n
Injustice, 125

Jealousy, 68, 115
Jesus brotherhood, 196, 261
Jesus Christ (Christ Michael)
  character of, 133, 148, 153, 250
  communication with, 177
  concentration on fundamentals by, 22–23, 86
  constraints of time on, 257
  on divine spirit, 33
  as expression of grace, 95
  and faith, 182
  family life of, 162, 163, 165–166, 176–177
  firsthand knowledge of, 81
  God's aid through, 101
  good news of, 28
  humanity of, 24, 27–28, 176–177
  imitation of, 154–155
  infancy of, 165–166
  joy of, 114
  knowledge of God, 177
  life of, 2, 5–6, 7, 9–10
  as listener, 20–21, 206, 208, 250
  living gospel of, 234
  meditation by, 54, 58
  and new Urantia lessons, 5
  obedience of, 93–94
  personal ministry of, 20, 223, 250
  practice as necessity for, 24
  on presence of God, 15
  proof of our worth through, 136
  religious life of, 27
  resurrection of, 27, 28
  sacrificial death of, 25–26, 112
  seeking of Father's will by, 58, 86
  on spiritual authority, 14–15
  teaching of fatherly love, 135
  teachings of, 5–6, 9–10, 191, 81
  in *The Urantia Book,* 5–6, 9–10
  view of family, 160
  visualization of, 182
  way of teaching of, 20, 128, 183, 202, 240, 250
Jesus Papers, 9–10
Joseph (father of Jesus), 24, 162, 164–166
Joy
  in faith, 114, 117
  in present moment, 156
  in service, 142, 218
  of simplicity, 142
Justice, and Father's love, 70

Kindness
  toward family, 167
  opportunities for, 198–199
  presence of God in, 48
Kingdom of Heaven, 15, 28, 151, 229, 238
Knowledge
  fragmentation of, 212
  of God, 64, 104, 115, 177, 210
  quest for, 156
  vs. truth, 212

Last Supper, 135
Laws of spiritual progress, 36
Leadership
  and Earth changes, 264
  and individual action, 197
  spiritual, 40, 259
Life, constraints of time on, 257
Light
  in daily life, 152–153
  sharing of, 142
  shepherds of, 245

# How to Find Out More About The Urantia Book and the Urantia Movement

*The Urantia Book* is universally available in bookstores and through booksellers on the World Wide Web (including our own website, www.IntegralSpirit.com). Below is an incomplete list of organizations devoted to the study and application of the teachings of *The Urantia Book*. (Note: These organizations have no affiliation with Origin Press or the Teaching Mission.)

**The Urantia Foundation**
533 Diversey Parkway
Chicago, IL 60614
773-525-3319
www.Urantia.org

The Urantia Foundation is the owner of the copyright to the original Urantia text, and is charged with the work of publishing the book, disseminating its teachings, and translating it into foreign languages. It sponsors the International Urantia Association, a worldwide educational association of readers that convenes study groups and conferences. The Urantia Foundation has no official connection with the Teaching Mission or related activities.

***The Urantia Book* Fellowship**
529 West Wrightwood Avenue
Chicago, IL 60614
773-327-0424
www.ubfellowship.org

*The Urantia Book* Fellowship is a social and educational organization whose purpose is to facilitate the worldwide dissemination of *The Urantia Book,* to stimulate study, and to help readers come into fellowship with one another through study groups and conferences. The Fellowship's website is a rich source of information related to the Urantia revelation. The Fellowship, through its publishing activity, Uversa Press, also produces numerous periodicals of interest to readers, notably the *Fellowship Forum,* the *Mighty Messenger,* and *The Study Group Herald.* (An independent website created by Fellowship members and other interested Urantians is www.ubook.org.)

## Good Cheer Catalog
P.O. Box 18764
Boulder, CO 80308
800-767-5683

The *Good Cheer Catalog,* published by the Jesusonian Foundation, is a key resource for the Urantia community worldwide. This catalog contains the widest variety of secondary sources related to the Urantia revelation, as well as discounted copies of all versions and all translations of *The Urantia Book.* (Many of these secondary works can also be obtained on-line at www.instantech.com/Urantia, an independent website not affiliated with the Jesusonian Foundation.)

## The School of Meanings and Values
P.O. Box 3324
Camarillo, CA 93011-3324

The School of Meanings and Values is devoted to the in-depth study of *The Urantia Book* and to training teachers and leaders in the ideals and philosophy of Jesus for worldwide service.

# VISIT WWW.INTEGRALSPIRIT.COM
## THE NEW WEBSITE FOR
## INTEGRAL SPIRITUALITY AND CULTURE

*The Urantia Book* is a key feature of a website created by Origin Press on the theme of integral spirituality and culture. Essays about the Urantia revelation and many other subjects can be found at the site; it also contains a selection of Teaching Mission transcripts. Features of the site include:

**Integral Spirit Journal**—columnists, essayists, and spiritual reviews of books and movies.

**Kosmos Cafe**—on-line virtual coffeehouse for integral visionaries, including a forum on the Urantia revelation.

**Visionary Arts Galley**—inspired fine art by leading visionary artists of our time.

**Kosmos Bookstore**—on-line bookstore for the spiritual community, including copies of *The Urantia Book* at 40% off.

**OriginPress.com**—Origin is the publishing house for books on integral spirituality.

# How to Find Out More About The Teaching Mission

To join a study group in your area based on *The Center Within,* or to receive notices about upcoming books in our series on the Teaching Mission, please write to:

1122 Grant Ave., Suite C
Novato, CA 94945
info@Originbooks.com
www.OriginPress.com
or call us at 1-888-267-4446

***The Light and Life Journal*** is a quarterly publication inspired by the Teaching Mission and *The Urantia Book* whose mission is the "exploration of the spiritual universe." This informative magazine is available on-line at **www.lightandlife.com**.

**The Stillness Foundation** is a membership organization inspired by the Teaching Mission that assists individuals in developing a personal relationship with God, and places special emphasis on teaching stillness meditation and related spiritual practices. The Foundation publishes books and tapes and presents workshops.

The Stillness Foundation
7840 Harcourt Springs Place
Indianapolis, IN 46260
317-334-1733

Transcripts of Teaching Mission lessons can be downloaded from the site **www.Spiritfest.com**. This website contains key information and resources related to the Mission, including a variety of e-mail groups, as well as other World Wide Web links of related interest.

# OTHER BOOKS BY FRED HARRIS
# BASED ON
# THE TEACHING MISSION

### *Correcting Time*

by Fred Harris

A fictional account of one man's transformation
in the early years of the Teaching Mission—
and his extraordinary encounters along the way.

### *Lessons for Personal Enlightenment:*
### *A Teaching Mission Daybook*

by Will & Company
edited by Fred Harris

These books are available from:
Mind, Body & Spirit, Inc.
P.O. Drawer 1838
Tallahassee, FL 32302
e-mail: harrisf606@aol.com

# GIVE THE GIFT OF
# THE CENTER WITHIN
## TO YOUR FRIENDS

## ORDER FORM

❏ Yes, I want _____ copies of *The Center Within* at $14.95 each
plus $3.50 shipping for the first book and $1.00 for each
additional book. California residents add 7¼% sales tax.

Name _____

Company_____

Address_____

City_____ State_____ Zip _____

Phone _____

Total  $_____

❏ Check or money order enclosed

Please charge my     ❏ Visa     ❏ MasterCard

Card #_____ Exp._____

Signature_____

**Call our Toll Free order line: 1-888-267-4446**
**Fax your order to: 415-898-1434**
**Order on-line: www.originpress.com**

Please make your check payable and return to:
Origin Press
1122 Grant Avenue, Suite C
Novato, California 94945

# THE
# CENTER WITHIN

LESSONS FROM THE HEART
OF THE URANTIA REVELATION

Compiled and Edited by
**Fred Harris and Byron Belitsos**

ⓧ ORIGIN PRESS

Origin Press
1122 Grant Ave., Suite C
Novato, CA 94945
888 267-4446

Cover art by Chuck Thurston, Boulder, CO.
Cover and text design by Lynn Bell, Monroe Street Studios, Santa Rosa, CA.

ISBN: 1-57983-001-3

*Library of Congress Cataloging-in-Publication Data*
Harris, Fred, and Belitsos, Byron.
    The center within : lessons from the heart of the Urantia revelation /
    compiled and edited by Fred Harris and Byron Belitsos.
        p.      cm.
    Includes index.
    ISBN 1-57983-003-X (softcover)
    1. Urantia book.    2. Urantia Foundation.    I. Harris, Fred, 1953–    .
    II. Belitsos, Byron, 1953–    .
    BP605.U75C46  1998                  98-23770
    299—dc21                            CIP

PRINTED IN THE UNITED STATES OF AMERICA ON RECYCLED PAPER

10 9 8 7 6 5 4 3 2 1